Following
God's Plan
For Your Life

FOLLOWING GOD'S PLAN FOR YOUR LIFE

Kenneth E. Hagin

Unless otherwise indicated, all Scripture quotations in this volume are from the *King James Version* of the Bible.

Sixth Printing 1996

ISBN 0-89276-519-4

In the U.S. write:
Kenneth Hagin Ministries
P.O. Box 50126
Tulsa, OK 74150-0126

In Canada write:
Kenneth Hagin Ministries
P.O. Box 335, Station D,
Etobicoke (Toronto), Ontario
Canada, M9A 4X3

BOOKS BY KENNETH E. HAGIN

* Redeemed From Poverty, Sickness and Spiritual Death
* What Faith Is
* Seven Vital Steps To Receiving the Holy Spirit
* Right and Wrong Thinking
  Prayer Secrets
* Authority of the Believer (foreign only)
* How To Turn Your Faith Loose
  The Key to Scriptural Healing
  Praying To Get Results
  The Present-Day Ministry of Jesus Christ
  The Gift of Prophecy
  Healing Belongs to Us
  The Real Faith
  How You Can Know the Will of God
  The Threefold Nature of Man
  The Human Spirit
  Turning Hopeless Situations Around
  Casting Your Cares Upon the Lord
  Seven Steps for Judging Prophecy
* The Interceding Christian
  Faith Food for Autumn
* Faith Food for Winter
  Faith Food for Spring
  Faith Food for Summer
* New Thresholds of Faith
* Prevailing Prayer to Peace
* Concerning Spiritual Gifts
  Bible Faith Study Course
  Bible Prayer Study Course
  The Holy Spirit and His Gifts
* The Ministry Gifts (Study Guide)
  Seven Things You Should Know About Divine Healing
  El Shaddai
  Zoe: The God-Kind of Life
  A Commonsense Guide to Fasting
  Must Christians Suffer?
  The Woman Question
  The Believer's Authority
  Ministering to Your Family
  What To Do When Faith Seems Weak and Victory Lost
  Growing Up, Spiritually
  Bodily Healing and the Atonement (Dr. T.J. McCrossan)
  Exceedingly Growing Faith
  Understanding the Anointing
  I Believe in Visions
  Understanding How To Fight the Good Fight of Faith
  Plans, Purposes, and Pursuits
  How You Can Be Led by the Spirit of God
  A Fresh Anointing
  Classic Sermons
  He Gave Gifts Unto Men:
     A Biblical Perspective of Apostles, Prophets, and Pastors
  The Art of Prayer
  Following God's Plan For Your Life

The Triumphant Church: Dominion Over All the Powers of Darkness
Healing Scriptures
Mountain-Moving Faith
Love: The Way to Victory
Biblical Keys to Financial Prosperity
The Price Is Not Greater Than God's Grace (Mrs. Oretha Hagin)

MINIBOOKS (A partial listing)

* The New Birth
* Why Tongues?
* In Him
* God's Medicine
* You Can Have What You Say
* Don't Blame God
* Words
  Plead Your Case
* How To Keep Your Healing
  The Bible Way To Receive the Holy Spirit
  I Went to Hell
  How To Walk in Love
  The Precious Blood of Jesus
* Love Never Fails
  How God Taught Me About Prosperity

BOOKS BY KENNETH HAGIN JR.

* Man's Impossibility — God's Possibility
  Because of Jesus
  How To Make the Dream God Gave You Come True
  The Life of Obedience
  Forget Not!
  God's Irresistible Word
  Healing: Forever Settled
  Don't Quit! Your Faith Will See You Through
  The Untapped Power in Praise
  Listen to Your Heart
  What Comes After Faith?
  Speak to Your Mountain!
  Come Out of the Valley!
  It's Your Move!
  God's Victory Plan
  Another Look at Faith

MINIBOOKS (A partial listing)

* Faith Worketh by Love
* Seven Hindrances to Healing
* The Past Tense of God's Word
  Faith Takes Back What the Devil's Stolen
  How To Be a Success in Life
  Get Acquainted With God
  Unforgiveness
  Ministering to the Brokenhearted

*These titles are also available in Spanish. Information about other foreign translations of several of the above titles (i.e., Finnish, French, German, Indonesian, Polish, Russian, etc.) may be obtained by writing to: Kenneth Hagin Ministries, P.O. Box 50126, Tulsa, Oklahoma 74150-0126.

Contents

Preface

Preface

We live in a day when we don't have time to play church or to fool around with the devil's games in our lives. The last days are upon us. The end of all things is at hand. Critical years lie ahead of us, for there is a great work to be done and a great harvest of souls to be reaped.

Never has it been so important for us to be free from all that has bound us in the past. Never has it been so crucial for us to be sensitive to the Holy Spirit's leading and for each of us to follow God's plan for our lives. It's time to shape up, friends. It's time to get serious about serving God and to be everything God wants us to be.

As you walk in obedience to God, your past failures and shortcomings which have hindered you from walking in the Spirit won't be able to keep what the Lord has ordained for you from coming to pass. If you do your part by preparing and obeying, all the carnal plans of man and all the demons in hell won't keep His plan from being fulfilled. *Nothing* will be able to detract or offset what God has proclaimed for your life!

"For I know the plans I have for you,"
declares the Lord,
"plans to prosper you
and not to harm you,
plans to give you hope and a future.

Then you will call upon me
and come and pray to me,
and I will listen to you.

You will seek me and find me
when you seek me with all your
heart."

— Jeremiah 29:11-13 (*NIV*)

*O Lord, that which I see not,
show Thou me.*

*That which I know not,
teach Thou me.*

*And that which Thou has
prepared for me,
prepare Thou me.*

Chapter 1
Running the Race

Wherefore seeing we also are COMPASSED ABOUT with so great a CLOUD OF WITNESSES, let us lay aside every weight, and the sin which doth so easily beset us, and let us RUN with patience THE RACE that is set before us.
— Hebrews 12:1

You have a particular race that God has set before *you* to run. It is a spiritual race that has to do with the divine destiny God has planned for you to fulfill. The Bible says you are not only to *run* your race, but you are to *finish* your race or course (2 Tim. 4:7). In other words, you are to fulfill God's plan and purpose for your own individual life. You are not to run *someone else's* race or finish *someone else's* course, for God has set a different course before each of us.

Why is it so important to follow God's plan for our lives? How can we successfully run our race and finish our course? The Bible answers these questions for us.

A Great Cloud of Witnesses

But first, notice something important in Hebrews 12:1. It says that we are not running our race unobserved. While we are running in this spiritual race, the Bible says we are "compassed about" by a "great cloud of witnesses."

1

Who is included in this great cloud of witnesses? Hebrews chapter 11 tells us. Remember, the writer of Hebrews (who I believe was Paul) did not write this letter to the Hebrew Christians in chapter and verse. So when we read Hebrews 12, we need to realize Paul was still talking about the "gallery of the heroes of faith" he had been discussing in Hebrews 11.

As Paul listed these heroes of faith in Hebrews 11, he began with Abel and then went on to talk about Enoch, Noah, Abraham and Sarah, Isaac, Jacob, Joseph, Moses, and so on. Then at the end of the chapter, Paul referred to all these heroes of faith, saying, *"And THESE ALL . . . obtained a good report through faith . . ."* (Heb. 11:39).

In the very next verse, Paul said, *"Wherefore seeing we also are compassed about with so great a CLOUD OF WITNESSES . . ."* (Heb. 12:1). So the men and women of faith Paul talked about in Hebrews 11 are a part of the cloud of witnesses Paul referred to in Hebrews 12:1.

What does Paul mean when he says we are "compassed about" by this cloud of witnesses? *The Living Bible* paraphrases it this way: "Since we have such a huge crowd of men [and women] of faith *watching us from the grandstands* . . . let us run with patience the particular race that God has set before us."

Paul used the illustration of running a race to describe how we are to follow God's plan for our lives in our Christian walk. He gave us the picture of the Grecian athletic games that were held in Paul's day, which were similar to our modern Olympic Games.

In the Grecian Games, those who ran in these races

were compassed about or surrounded by people watching them from the grandstands, cheering them on. So in Hebrews 12:1, Paul was saying in essence, "All these heroes I've listed here and all the other believers who have ever died are watching us from the grandstands in Heaven as we run our spiritual race."

That great cloud of witnesses in Heaven, as well as every believer on earth, are all a part of the family of God that Paul talks about in Ephesians 3:14 and 15: *"For this cause I bow my knees unto the Father of our Lord Jesus Christ, of whom the whole family in heaven and earth is named."* Let it encourage you to know you have family in Heaven's grandstands cheering you on as you run your race!

This huge crowd of men and women of faith are not watching you as you run your *natural* race on this earth. They are not interested in the natural things of life.

For example, they aren't watching you as you go about your daily business. They aren't interested in whether or not you bought new clothes or a new car or how much money you have in the bank. They are watching you in your Christian walk as you run your *spiritual* race. They are interested in whether or not you are following God's plan for your life.

I had a supernatural experience years ago which gave me this revelation and showed me the reality of the cloud of witnesses watching us from Heaven's grandstands.

At a seminar in 1968, Sister Jeanne Wilkerson, an established Bible teacher and prophetess (who has since gone on to be with the Lord), prophesied that in the fall of that year I would have an experience similar to Enoch's in that I would be caught up to Heaven. Enoch was caught away in the flesh — his physical body departed from this earth (Gen. 5:24; Heb. 11:5). But Sister Wilkerson prophesied that I would be caught away in the Spirit and would receive revelation from God.

I didn't do anything to try to make that prophecy come to pass. I just continued to serve God. Then in the fall of that year, my only sister, Oleta, died of cancer when she was only fifty-five years of age.

Oleta had been sick once before and had almost died. When I prayed for her, she was healed. She was a spiritual babe in Christ at that time, so I could get her healed on my faith in the Word. But this time when she got sick, she was no longer a spiritual baby, so I couldn't get her healed on my faith. We won't be able to carry other people on our faith indefinitely because God expects each of us to grow up in faith.

So my sister died in the fall of that year. In fact, our family was all gathered around my sister's bed on the evening she drew her last breath. About 1:30 the next morning, I was lying in bed thinking about what it must have been like for my sister as her spirit left her body, and she ascended to Heaven to be with the Lord.

I thought about the time my own heart stopped beating on August 16, 1933, as I lay on the bed of sickness. When my heart stopped, my spirit left my body, and as I looked back down, I could see my body lying there on the bed. I saw my mother holding my hand. Then I thought about my sister again. When she died and left her body, she must have looked down upon all of us gathered around her bed and seen our love and concern.

As I was thinking about this, suddenly a bright, golden beam of light from Heaven about as big as an elevator shaft penetrated right through the ceiling. When that light touched me, my spirit left my body. I went right up through that beam of light as if I were going up an elevator, until I reached Heaven.

In Heaven, I saw my sister talking to Jesus. When I walked up to them, Jesus stopped talking to her and looked at me. When Jesus looked at me, my sister turned around to see who Jesus was looking at and saw me.

The first thing my sister said to me was, "Ken, don't feel so badly that you couldn't pray the prayer of faith for me. There was a reason why you couldn't." (She didn't tell me what the reason was.)

Sometimes God doesn't reveal to us the reason why some people don't receive their healing. Deuteronomy 29:29 says, *"The secret things belong unto the Lord our God. . . ."*

My sister told me she had already seen Granny and Grandpa, my mother's parents. She also said she had seen her grandson, Jason, who had died when he was three years old. Then she said, "Kenneth, I saw Ann." Ann was her daughter who had died as a result of an automobile accident when she was only twenty-five years old, leaving behind two small children.

My sister continued, "The first thing Ann said to me was, 'How are Bill and the children?' (Bill was Ann's husband.) I didn't tell Ann that Bill had remarried."

Then my sister said something that came as a real revelation to me. She told me, "You see, people up here are not interested in the natural side of life of those living on the earth. They are not concerned about whether or not you buy a new dress or a new suit, or how much money you have in the bank.

"They are concerned about *spiritual* things. They don't know what happens in your life in the natural realm, but they know everything you do spiritually. They know when you make a decision for Christ."

My sister was talking about the cloud of witnesses in Heaven watching us as we run our spiritual race. That was the revelation Sister Wilkerson had prophesied I would receive during this experience. Before this experience of being caught up to Heaven, I'd only had a hint or glimpse of that revelation.

My sister also said to me, "Ken, please talk to ____ (and she mentioned the name of her youngest son). He'll listen to you."

The son my sister was talking about had known God at one time and had the call of God on his life to the ministry. But then he ran away from God and hadn't been in fellowship with God for many years.

My sister said, "Tell my son I told you that he will never be happy, and life will never go right with him until he surrenders his life to the Lord. Tell him when he rededicates his life to the Lord, I will know it. We know up here what goes on spiritually on the earth."

After this experience, I did talk to my sister's son as she had asked me to. Although he made a move toward God at the time, he didn't fully surrender his life to God. Because of that, just as my sister predicted, nothing seemed to go right in his life for many years after that.

Then during one of our recent Campmeetings, my sister's son completely surrendered his life to the Lord and answered the call on his life to the ministry! Thank God, my sister knew in Heaven the moment her son rededicated his life to Jesus. She is rejoicing as he now endeavors to run his race and follow God's plan for his life!

Incidentally, when Sister Wilkerson prophesied that I would be caught up to Heaven like Enoch and receive revelation, she also said that another person would be involved in a similar supernatural experience. My older brother, Dub, was that person. The same night I was caught up to Heaven, Dub had a similar experience. Dub was also caught up to Heaven and had a conversation with our sister, just as I had a short time earlier.

At the time this happened to Dub, no one could have accused him of being spiritual! Dub didn't understand much about spiritual things, and his experience in Heaven unnerved him. He called me the next day to tell me about it. He had no idea I'd had a similar experience the same night.

Dub told me, "When I went up to Heaven, I saw Sis. She was talking to Jesus, and she looked so pretty. She said to me, 'Dub, you talk to ____ (and she mentioned her oldest son). He won't listen to anyone but you.'" My sister's oldest son had also fallen away from the Lord.

Dub did talk to Oleta's oldest son. And although the young man didn't make a decision when Dub talked to him, he did recommit his life to the Lord later on and is serving the Lord today.

I'm relating this experience I had in Heaven in order to make Hebrews 12:1 a little more real to you. My sister is just one in that great cloud of witnesses who is watching us from Heaven's grandstands. And the Apostle Paul and other patriarchs of the Bible are also a part of that great company watching us. The other apostles — Peter, James, and John — are watching us too! They are all watching us as we run our spiritual race!

If you have any loved ones who have gone home to be with the Lord, you can rest assured that they're watching *you* as you run your race. They are cheering you on as you follow God's plan for your life, because they want to see you finish your course.

I remember watching my son, Ken, in a high school track meet. I was in the grandstands close to the track, and as Ken came running around the track near me, I started cheering him on. A runner was closing in behind Ken, so I hollered, "Run, Ken! He's catching you!" Ken could hear me cheering him on, and I watched him as he seemed to gather strength from deep inside. He quickened his pace until he was twenty yards in front of every other runner!

My son's team won first place in that relay race. Knowing his dad was cheering him on helped Ken do his best in that race. In the same way, we can determine to do our best to run our spiritual race while our family in Heaven's grandstands cheers us on to finish the course God has set before each of us!

Lay Aside Every Weight

So how do we run our race in such a way that God's plan will be fulfilled in our lives and Heaven will rejoice? Look again at Hebrews 12:1: *". . . let us LAY ASIDE EVERY WEIGHT, and the SIN which doth so easily beset us, and let us RUN WITH PATIENCE the race that is set before us."*

The Living Bible gives us a clearer picture of what it means to "lay aside every weight and sin."

HEBREWS 12:1 *(Living Bible)*
1 Since we have such a huge crowd of men of faith watching us from the grandstands, let us STRIP OFF ANYTHING that SLOWS US DOWN or HOLDS US BACK, and especially those SINS that WRAP THEMSELVES SO TIGHTLY AROUND OUR FEET and TRIP US UP; and let us run with patience the particular race that God has set before us.

Think about the way a runner dresses in an actual Olympic race. He doesn't run with an overcoat on, does he? And he doesn't run with all his street clothes on. Why? Because that would slow him down. Also, a runner doesn't wait until he's run half the race before he pulls off his overcoat, saying, "This coat is holding me back." If he did that, there's no way he could win the race!

In the natural, wearing an overcoat would slow a runner down and keep him from winning his race. It's the same way in the spiritual realm. Sin will slow you down, it will keep tripping you up, and it can prevent you from running your spiritual race.

You see, sin in your life will not only hinder your fellowship with God, it will dull your spirit and cause you to be less responsive to the Holy Spirit's leading. Therefore, sin left unchecked will cause you to live only in the natural realm, and you'll miss God's best for your life.

It is also easy to become too entangled with *legiti-mate* affairs of life — things which may be good in themselves but are not what God has called *you* to do. There are many things in this life that are not neces-sarily wrong, but they will slow you down in *your* par-ticular spiritual race. They will hinder you from growing spiritually and from fulfilling God's purposes in your life.

That's why God tells us in Hebrews 12:1 to strip off those weights and sins in our lives that are tripping us up and slowing us down spiritually. And we should strip them off *now* so we are not hindered from fulfill-ing the plan of God for our lives. If we wait to strip off those weights until we have plodded slowly through half our race, we risk the possibility of never finishing our course and not fulfilling the plan of God for our lives (2 Tim. 4:7).

Notice Hebrews 12:1 says *you* are the one who must strip off the weights and sins that hinder you and hold you back in your Christian walk. Of course, God will help you. The Holy Spirit, the Helper, dwells within you to give you the power and ability to obey God (John 14:26 *Amp.*). But God is not going to pull off your "coat" — those weights and sins that slow you down — and lay them aside *for* you! *You* are going to have to do it.

That's why some people have trouble running their spiritual race; they are not stripping off everything that would slow them down or hold them back. They are not laying aside the sin that "wraps itself so tightly around their feet and trips them up."

Another reason people sometimes have trouble running their spiritual race is that they are not running the race God told *them* to run. They are not following *His* plan or *His* purpose for their lives. When that happens, their race can become hard and burdensome to run.

But God doesn't want the race He has set before us to be difficult and burdensome.

MATTHEW 11:28-30
28 Come unto me, all ye that labour and are heavy laden, and I will give you rest.
29 Take my yoke upon you, and learn of me; for I am meek and lowly in heart: and ye shall find rest unto your souls.
30 For MY YOKE IS EASY, and MY BURDEN IS LIGHT.

Often the difficulties we face in running our race are not the result of *God's* yoke upon us or trying to fulfill *His* will for our lives. Many times the difficulties we encounter are the result of what *we* have failed to do by not stripping off everything that would hinder us.

So in the same way you might take your coat off and throw it down, make the decision to strip off every wrong motive, every selfish ambition, carnal inclination, and desire of the flesh that will hinder you in your race.

Lay aside weights and sins like pride, double-mindedness, spiritual slothfulness, and fear. Cast all these weights and sins far from you and refuse to take them up again. You must do this if you want to do your best to run your spiritual race and finish your course with joy.

Running Our Race With Patience

Now let's look at the last part of Hebrews 12:1:
*". . . let us run WITH PATIENCE the race that is set
before us."* We can also make our way difficult and hinder our spiritual growth if we do not run the race set
before us with *patience*. Running our race with patience
can be a challenge. It is so easy to become impatient in
our desire to see God's plans and purposes fulfilled in
our lives.

For example, humans can be so time-conscious.
Many times when we hear from the Lord regarding His
plan for us, we want it to be fulfilled *immediately*. But
we need to learn patience as we run our spiritual race.

You see, God doesn't operate in the realm of time.
The Bible says that one day is as a thousand years with
the Lord (2 Peter 3:8). God knows no time, no hours, no
days, no years. What may seem like a great length of
time to us may be only a fleeting moment from God's
perspective. That's why it's so important to learn to rest
in the promises of God's Word without regard to time
limits. When we learn to enter into the rest of faith, we
give the Lord the freedom to bring His plan to pass in
our lives.

Sometimes when God says something to believers
about His plans for their lives, they try to make it come
to pass by their own efforts. When they do that, they
can muddy the waters, so to speak. What do I mean by
that? In other words, they can hinder God's plan for
them so God isn't free to do what He wants to do. They
need to just stay in faith regarding God's plan and let

God bring to pass what He has told them. To fulfill *their* part, they need to prepare themselves according to the Word and the Holy Spirit's leading.

I muddied the waters of God's plan for me more than once when I was young in the Lord. Sometimes when the Lord said something to me about my ministry, I would try to jump out immediately and do it. Every single time I did that, what the Lord told me to do didn't work out right.

Now someone might think, *Well, that just shows that the Lord didn't really speak to you.* But the Lord *did* speak to me; I just didn't get the timing right, so I hindered God's plan.

Jesus told me once when He appeared to me in a vision, "I'd rather you were too slow than too fast when you are trying to follow My leading. At least when you're behind Me, you can still see Me out ahead of you. But if you're too fast and you jump out ahead of Me, you won't be able to see Me any longer, and you'll get off track."

As I grew in the Lord, I learned not to jump out ahead of Him, but to just allow Him to bring to pass His purposes for me as I stayed faithful to prepare myself. I also learned not only to get the *what* of God's plan, but to continue to pray until I have the *when* and the *how*.

You see, just because the Lord says something to you doesn't mean He wants you to do it *immediately*. And it doesn't mean He wants you to do it next week, next month, or even next year. That is absolutely the truth.

God has prepared a plan for your life, but you aren't always ready to fulfill the next step of that plan. So God will take whatever time is needed to develop and train you before He brings to pass what He has spoken to your heart.

Preparing for His Purposes

Days of preparation are never lost time. There may be important lessons or truths that you still need to learn in order to successfully fulfill God's plan for you. And it takes time to prepare and establish yourself in God's Word (2 Tim. 2:15).

However, going through a time of preparation is not always easy, for sometimes there is a price to be paid. From your perspective, your preparation time might not always be comfortable because you might have to die to your own desires and *your* timing as you allow God to prepare you.

So although it may seem difficult or uncomfortable, preparation is a part of the race God has set before you to run. And it pays to be faithful during the time of preparation, even if it means there will be some sacrifice on your part. For when you are thoroughly prepared and you have proven to God that He can trust you, He will be able to promote you and move you into the place He had planned for you all along — a place of greater responsibility, anointing, and ministry.

However, if you don't prepare yourself during your preparation time, you won't be ready to take the next step in God's plan for you. If you've neglected your time of training and only concerned yourself with natural affairs, then when God's door of opportunity opens, you may not even recognize it. And if you haven't prepared

yourself, you won't be ready to go through that door
into the next stage of God's plan for you.

You see, often our spiritual race is like a relay race
in the natural. In a relay race, the runner races until he
reaches a certain station, and then he hands the baton
to the next runner.

In much the same way, there are often different
stages to the Christian race, and there are usually
times of preparation before each new stage. Often our
own obedience every step of the way and our faithfulness to prepare ourselves in the Word determine how
long the time is between one stage and the next or if we
ever reach the next stage.

Many times folks hear from God regarding the next
stage in their race and just assume they are supposed
to act right away on what He told them to do. But
because they are not ready or they have not fully prepared themselves as they should have, when they step
out to do what God told them to do, it doesn't work out
right, and they fall flat on their faces. You see, God has
a *way*, but He also has a *timing*. And to move out of
God's timing is to move out of His will.

Moses is a biblical example of someone who jumped
out ahead of God's timing and muddied the waters of
God's plan. While Moses lived in Pharaoh's palace in
Egypt, he sensed the call of God on his life to deliver
Israel from slavery. But God's plan of deliverance may
have been delayed because Moses jumped out ahead of
God's timing and tried to make it happen in his own
way and in his own strength.

When Moses was forty years old, he killed an Egyptian who was beating a Hebrew slave. That was *not* God's plan or His way to deliver Israel!

News of what Moses did spread quickly. When Pharaoh heard what Moses had done, he sought to kill him. Moses had to run for his life to the wilderness (Exod. 2:11-15).

It took a long time of living on the back side of the desert for Moses to learn enough patience so God could use him to fulfill the divine plan of Israel's deliverance. It was forty years later when God finally told Moses it was time to deliver the Israelites from the hands of the Egyptians.

I can also give you an example from my own life of stepping out ahead of God. By the mid-1940s, God had already put in my heart much of what I am doing today in my ministry. I knew in my spirit God had something besides pastoring that He wanted me to do.

So in 1944, I left the church I was pastoring to go into field ministry, thinking God's timing was *right then* for the next phase of my ministry to begin. But I jumped into the field ministry out of God's timing. Therefore, things didn't work out right.

Don't misunderstand me; God blessed my year in field ministry as much as He could. We had some good meetings, and people got saved and baptized in the Holy Spirit. But I knew I had stepped out prematurely into the next stage of God's plan for me. So I backed up to where I had missed it and went back to pastoring.

Although God really had talked to me at that time about my ministry, it wasn't time yet for those things to come to pass. For example, God's timing for what He had put in my heart about going into the field ministry was five years later. (Some of what He told me came to pass *much* later, and some of it is *still* coming to pass!)

By the time five more years had passed, I had learned enough to say, "This time I'm not moving unless I get the witness in my spirit that it's time to move." So I continued to pastor my last church until the Holy Spirit quickened to my spirit in early 1949 that it was time to move out into the field ministry.

Over the years I've learned to operate that way in every area of my life. I don't move until I get the signal from the Holy Spirit to move. When I get that signal and act on what God has told me, I have found that God's plan always works smoothly.

For example, I'm doing things today in our ministry that God told me to do many years ago. But just because I heard from God back then, I didn't immediately act on what He told me to do. If I had immediately acted on what God had told me to do, I would have moved out of His timing. The ministry would have suffered, and that part of God's plan for me would have been greatly hindered.

But instead, I waited until I received the signal in my spirit when to act on God's plan. Then I acted on what I knew in my spirit. Because I waited, each time I acted on something God told us to do, it worked so smoothly, it amazed me. That's because I moved according to God's plan *in His timing*.

I learned long ago not to try to figure out *in my own natural understanding* how and when God's plan will come to pass. For instance, during my last three years of pastoring in the late '40s, I waited upon God in prayer for hours and days at a time seeking Him and His will for my life. As I waited upon God, I saw in the Spirit different aspects of my ministry, which have only come to pass in recent years.

However, I didn't see the whole picture of what my ministry would involve. At that stage of my spiritual development, if I had known then what would be happening today in my ministry, it would have scared me! God doesn't tell us His whole plan for us all at once. Often He can tell us only bits and pieces of His plan because we wouldn't be able to understand or bear more than a glimpse of what He has in store for us (John 16:12).

I had no idea how God was going to fulfill what He had shown me regarding my ministry, so I just left the whole matter in His hands. And as I've been faithful to obey Him step by step, in His own time He has brought to pass what He revealed to me more than forty years ago.

A person has to be patient to wait for *God* to bring to pass His purpose in his life. There is a time and a season for all things (Eccl. 3:1), and the time is not always *now*. That's why the Bible says, ". . . *let us run with PATIENCE the race that is set before us*" (Heb. 12:1).

Someone might say, "But will things ever change? I know that God is preparing me, and I want to be faithful. But it seems that I've been in this place of preparation for such a long time. Will it ever be different?"

Just continue to trust in the Lord with all your heart and to run your race with patience. Don't try to *figure out* how and when God is going to fulfill His plan for you; pray about it, and as you need to know, He will reveal each step you need to take. Just learn to rest in faith and to flow with the Holy Spirit.

Be content to be faithful and trust God to alert your spirit when it's time to take the next step in His plan for you. Let *God* be the One to accomplish His will in your life. Then when it is time to move on to the next stage in His plan for you, you'll be thoroughly furnished — not just half prepared — to do what He has called you to do.

You need to realize that you won't come into the full potential of what God has prepared for you tomorrow or next week or next month. But as you are faithful to prepare yourself and as you learn to yield to the Holy Spirit's leading, you will step into what God has planned for you.

You won't step into the fullness of God's plan immediately as you would step through a door. But gradually, little by little, as you're faithful and obedient, you will keep moving toward God's destiny for you. And one day you will finally stand in the full-fledged orb of God's blessings and His purpose for your life. Once you do reach that stage, you'll look back on your time of preparation and say, "Thank God for those days of preparation! Thank God I was faithful to obey God!"

As you run your race with patience, remember also that you are not to try to run someone else's race. Don't look around to see where others are in their race and then try to get on their track to run. Let God speak to *you* where you are at in your race.

Find the race that God has set before *you*. Strip off the weights and sins that would hinder you from obeying God. Then run *your* race with your eyes set on the goal — the prize of the high calling of God in Christ Jesus (Phil. 3:14). Determine to follow God's plan for your life and to *finish* your course with joy.

Chapter 2
Maintaining a Spirit-Filled Life

Wherefore be ye not unwise, BUT UNDER-STANDING WHAT THE WILL [or purpose] *OF THE LORD IS.*

And be not drunk with wine, wherein is excess; but BE FILLED WITH THE SPIRIT;

Speaking to yourselves in psalms and hymns and spiritual songs, singing and making melody in your heart to the Lord;

Giving thanks always for all things unto God and the Father in the name of our Lord Jesus Christ;

Submitting yourselves one to another in the fear of God.

— Ephesians 5:17-21

Be kindly affectioned one to another with brotherly love; in honour preferring one another;

Not slothful in business; FERVENT IN SPIRIT; serving the Lord.

— Romans 12:10,11

Many Christians struggle in life wondering what the

will of God is for their lives. God does impart specific direction to His people concerning His plans and purposes for their lives. But even in those times when God doesn't seem to be saying anything specific to them about His plan, believers can know and do the will of God in their everyday lives simply by being doers of the *Word.*

Notice our text says, *"Wherefore be ye not unwise, but UNDERSTANDING WHAT THE WILL OF THE LORD IS. And be not drunk with wine, wherein is excess; but BE FILLED WITH THE SPIRIT"* (Eph. 5:17,18). These verses are telling us that it is possible to know what the will of the Lord is for our lives. For one thing, God's will is that believers be filled to overflowing with His Spirit.

How can you tell if a person is filled with the Holy Ghost? Someone said, "I'm filled with the Holy Ghost because I spoke with tongues years ago."

But D. L. Moody once said, "Living only on past experiences is living on stale manna." I agree. Ephesians 5:18 says, *". . . be not drunk with wine, wherein is excess; but BE filled with the Spirit."* In other words, to *be* filled with the Spirit is to be filled *now* in the *present tense.* It's a continual, ongoing action, not something that occurred once sometime in the past.

Greek scholars tell us that in Ephesians 5:18, the Greek words for *"be filled* with the Spirit" mean be *being* filled with the Holy Spirit. In other words, we are to maintain a constant experience of being filled with the Holy Spirit. The will of God for our lives is that we be filled to overflowing with the Holy Spirit.

Notice the expression in Romans 12:11 "fervent in spirit." Another translation says, "Have your spirits aglow" (*Weymouth*). *The Revised Standard Version* says, "Be aglow with the Spirit."

The *Moffatt's* translation says, "Maintain the glow." I like that one best. That's the will of the Lord for our lives. In other words, that's what He wants us to do: Maintain the glow of the Holy Spirit. Being filled with the Spirit and maintaining the glow is God's *will* for us because it's written in His *Word*. And we know that God's *Word* is God's *will*.

> **HEBREWS 1:1,2**
> 1 God, who at sundry times and in divers manners spake in time past unto the fathers by the prophets,
> 2 Hath in these last days SPOKEN UNTO US BY HIS SON, whom he hath appointed heir of all things. . . .

The Bible is God speaking to us personally. And the Bible says it is God's will for us to "be fervent in spirit" or to *maintain the glow* of the Holy Spirit (Rom. 12:11). Another translation of Romans 12:11 says, "Be on fire with the Spirit" (*Goodspeed*).

Romans 1:7 says, *"To all that be in Rome, beloved of God, called to be saints. . . ."* The Apostle Paul wrote the Epistle of Romans to the Church at Rome, but it applies to every one of us who belongs to the Church of the Lord Jesus Christ, wherever we might be. God wants each of us to maintain a Spirit-filled life and be fervent in spirit or *maintain the glow*.

Maintaining a Spirit-filled life is as much a part of following God's plan for your life as receiving specific direction from the Lord about something He wants you to do. For example, you could receive specific direction from God about part of His plan for you, and you could obey it. But if you obeyed His direction strictly from a sense of duty, it still wouldn't be God's best for your life. There would be no fervency of spirit or glow about it, and it would be tough sledding! In other words, God's will for your life would be difficult to fulfill.

No, God wants you to be filled to overflowing with His Spirit and maintain the glow! *That's* God's will — His purpose — for your life, because God knows that when you are filled to overflowing with His Spirit, it will be much easier to successfully follow His plan for your life.

Maintaining the Glow Is Recognizable

According to Ephesians 5:18-21, being filled with the Spirit or being fervent in spirit is recognizable. If it weren't recognizable, you wouldn't know whether or not you were aglow with the Holy Spirit.

In Acts 6:1-3, we see men who were chosen to do a work for God because they were filled to overflowing with the Holy Spirit. They were aglow with the Spirit, and it was recognizable.

ACTS 6:1-3
1 And in those days, when the number of the disciples was multiplied, there arose a murmuring of

**the Grecians against the Hebrews, because their
widows were neglected in the daily ministration.
2 Then the twelve called the multitude of the disciples unto them, and said, It is not reason that we
should leave the word of God, and serve tables.
3 Wherefore, brethren, look ye out among you
seven men OF HONEST REPORT, FULL OF THE
HOLY GHOST AND WISDOM, whom we may
appoint over this business.**

In the beginning of the Church at Jerusalem, the
believers shared all things in common (Acts 2:44). The
apostles were overseeing the Church and had both natural and spiritual duties to carry out. When some of the
people felt that they were being neglected in the daily
ministration of food, the apostles said to the disciples,
*". . . It is not reason that we should leave the word of
God, and serve tables . . . look ye out among you seven
men of HONEST REPORT . . ."* (Acts 6:2,3).

All the money had been pooled into one treasury, so
the apostles needed someone to take care of the money
as well as to serve tables. The apostles wanted seven
men who had an honest report. They *sure* didn't want
people handling the money who didn't have an honest
reputation!

The disciples didn't look out in the world among sinners for seven honest men; they looked among *Christians.* Isn't it strange that among believers they'd have
to say, "Look for those who are honest"? Evidently, there
were some in the Church who didn't have a reputation
for being honest!

An honest report was something the disciples were

looking for. In other words, a person's honesty and integrity are recognizable. These qualities can be *seen* or *recognized* in a person's life.

Notice the second characteristic the disciples were to look for in choosing seven men to assist them: "... *look ye out among you seven men* ... *FULL OF THE HOLY GHOST*..." (Acts 6:3).

In much the same way an honest reputation is recognizable, being filled to overflowing with the Holy Ghost is also recognizable. When believers are filled to overflowing with the Holy Spirit, they are fervent in spirit or on fire with the Holy Spirit.

The third characteristic the disciples were looking for was *wisdom* (v. 3). They needed men who were honest and full of the Holy Ghost. But without wisdom, especially in dealing with money, the men they chose could have gotten the business affairs of the church in a mess.

Notice how this passage in Acts 6 ties in with Romans 12:11: *"NOT SLOTHFUL IN BUSINESS; fervent in spirit; serving the Lord."* The phrase "not slothful in business" means not being slothful in handling financial affairs.

That's the reason some Christians are in a mess financially — they don't have any wisdom. Believers could receive the baptism in the Holy Spirit and still lack wisdom, and they would get things in a mess.

In fact, without wisdom, you could get into trouble spiritually, mentally, physically, and financially. Without wisdom, you could get into trouble in your marriage, in other relationships, and in your ministry or on your job.

Without wisdom, you won't be able to successfully follow and fulfill God's plan for your life. But you don't have to lack wisdom. The Bible says we can have wisdom by simply asking God for it in faith (James 1:5). God wants to give you wisdom and cause you to prosper in every area of your life.

We saw in Acts 6:1-3 that the characteristics of honesty, wisdom, and being full of the Holy Ghost are characteristics that can be seen or recognized. In other words, you can tell whether or not a person is filled to overflowing with the Spirit, because certain characteristics accompany the Spirit-filled life.

The first characteristic of a Spirit-filled life is *"Speaking to yourselves in psalms and hymns and spiritual songs, singing and making melody in your heart to the Lord"* (Eph. 5:18).

If you're filled with the Spirit and you're maintaining the glow, you will have a song in your heart. And if you've got a song in your heart, you just can't help but speak it out of your mouth, because the Bible says that out of the abundance of the heart the mouth speaks (Matt. 12:34; Luke 6:45).

Notice Ephesians 5:18 says, *"Speaking to YOURSELVES in psalms and hymns and spiritual songs. . . ."* Speaking by the unction of the Holy Spirit in psalms, hymns, and spiritual songs is something you do from your own heart — to yourself and to God.

A psalm is a spiritual poem or an ode. It may rhyme or it may not rhyme, but there is always an element of poetry about it. There are 150 psalms in the Old Testament that were given by the Spirit of God. Many of them were given to the psalmist David by the gift of prophecy or the inspiration of the Holy Ghost. And if you'll read them carefully, you'll find out that many of them were given to David for his own benefit to encourage him in difficult circumstances.

Those psalms are also to benefit us today (2 Tim. 3:16). And just as those psalms were given to encourage David, the Holy Ghost will do the same thing for you! He'll give you a psalm to encourage you in the midst of tests and trials and to lift up your spirit so you can maintain the glow!

A psalm, hymn, or spiritual song can be a supernatural utterance given to you by the Holy Ghost. They don't have to be psalms, hymns, or songs written in a songbook. To tell you the real truth about it, so many songs in songbooks are not given by the Holy Ghost at all. They're not thoroughly scriptural, and some are filled with unbelief.

But the psalms, hymns, and spiritual songs the Holy Ghost gives register on your heart and minister to your soul because they are Holy Spirit inspired. And before you know it, you're singing or speaking them out of your mouth.

You see, you cannot be filled with the Spirit without *speaking.*

EPHESIANS 5:18,19
18 And be not drunk with wine, wherein is excess; but be FILLED WITH THE SPIRIT;
19 SPEAKING to yourselves in psalms and hymns

and spiritual songs, singing and making melody in your heart to the Lord.

ACTS 2:4
4 And they were all FILLED WITH THE HOLY GHOST, and began TO SPEAK with other tongues....

ACTS 10:45,46
45 And they of the circumcision which believed were astonished, as many as came with Peter, because that on the Gentiles also was POURED OUT the gift of THE HOLY GHOST.
46 For they heard them SPEAK WITH TONGUES, and MAGNIFY GOD....

So keep on speaking with tongues and magnifying God! And be continually filled with the Holy Spirit, speaking to yourself in psalms, hymns, and spiritual songs. *This* is the will of God for you.

Maintaining the Glow Will Affect You — Spirit , Soul, and Body

If you maintain a Spirit-filled life, it will greatly affect you in every area of your life. Of course, it will affect you spiritually, but it will also affect you mentally. As you maintain a Spirit-filled life, you'll be sharper and clearer in your thinking. And being filled to overflowing with the Holy Spirit will affect you physically too. *This* is the will of God for your life — to continually be aglow with the Spirit of God!

It's very easy to discern if someone is up to par

physically or mentally. For example, if someone is not feeling good, he's just not himself. He's not as sharp as he could be. You can tell by a person's countenance if he's tired or doesn't feel well.

Spiritual health is discernible too. In fact, a person's spiritual health is just as discernible as his physical health. One of the pioneers of the Pentecostal Movement who lived in Great Britain illustrated this point by a personal experience he once had.

This minister was a pastor in England when this happened. He had renewed acquaintances with a minister friend who had been on the mission field and had returned home for the first time in seven years. His minister friend arrived home by boat, so the pastor met him at port.

As soon as they exchanged greetings and began talking, the missionary looked at this pastor and asked, "What's wrong with you?"

"What do you mean by that?" the pastor replied and began to defend himself. "Nothing's wrong with me."

"You're not up to par spiritually," the missionary answered.

Later, this pastor thought, *He could tell something was wrong with me. Something is wrong; I'm not where I should be spiritually. But what's the problem?*

Then on the inside, in his own spirit, he had the answer. In a city of more than a million people, his church had been the only Full Gospel church. But then a fellow came along and started another work in the city, and he had gotten upset about it.

Some of his congregation began to go to the new Full Gospel church because it was closer to their homes. The pastor of the established church began harboring ill-will toward the other pastor because he thought the new pastor had invaded *his* territory.

But when did a city of more than one million people get to be *his* territory anyway? The Bible says the earth and the fullness thereof is the Lord's, not a certain minister's! Ministers should be *glad* when someone starts a new church in their city so more souls can be brought into God's Kingdom!

Don't misunderstand me. It is wrong, for example, for some minister to come to another man's church, steal his sheep, and go start another church down the street. That wouldn't be walking in love and putting the other fellow first. Ministers *should* have ethics and walk in love toward one another.

But on the other hand, you can get in a ditch on the other side of this issue too. For example, the pastor of the established church was only running 250 members in his church out of a citywide population of more than one million. The new church was started miles across town, yet the pastor of the established church got mad about it, and it affected him spiritually.

You see, your spirit knows more about spiritual things than your head knows. In his heart, this pastor knew where he had missed it with God. And when he realized his mistake, he went to the new pastor in the city and told him he loved and appreciated him and his ministry. Then he invited the new pastor to one of his church services. After that, the pastor of the established church got on fire for God again.

You see, there's a lot more to maintaining the Spirit-filled life than just jumping up and down and laughing and shouting in the Holy Ghost. Certainly, that's part of it, but there's a whole lot more to it than that. For example, you could get blessed in a service where the Spirit of God was in powerful manifestation, but that wouldn't mean that everything in your life is right on spiritually.

Maintaining the glow is maintaining your spiritual health. And that includes being filled to overflowing with the Spirit every day in your personal everyday life. That's what Paul meant when he said, *". . . be ye not unwise, but understanding what the will of the Lord is . . . be* [continually] *filled with the Spirit"* (Eph. 5:17,18). In other words, *maintain the glow!*

Many Christians are caught up trying to receive specific direction from God, but they forget to be a doer of the *Word*. But being a doer of God's Word is God's will just as much as obeying any specific direction they may receive from Him.

Walk in the Light of God's Word

For instance, God's Word says we should walk in love toward one another. That means to walk in love is God's will for our lives. The Bible says if we're not walking in love, we're not walking in the light (1 John 2:11).

Yet how many Christians miss it and fail to walk in the light of God's Word — *His will* — when it comes to walking in love! How can they expect to receive specific direction from God and follow His plan for their lives when they're walking in spiritual darkness and can't even see where they're going!

I remember an experience I had in the Farmersville church my wife and I pastored more than fifty years ago. We used to sing a chorus in Pentecostal circles: "Got any rivers you think are uncrossable? Got any mountains you can't tunnel through? God specializes in things thought impossible, And He can do what no other power can do."[1]

During one of the services in that Farmersville church, one of the deacons said, "Sing my favorite chorus," and everyone began to sing this song. As everyone sang, this deacon shouted and jumped up and down for joy. He was so happy, he almost jumped over a pew.

But on their way home right after the service, his wife mentioned to him that one of their sons needed a new pair of shoes. When she said that, this deacon just exploded, shouting, "Do you think I'm made out of money! We just bought him a pair of shoes a few months ago!"

Of course, this deacon wasn't considering that a growing boy could outgrow a pair of shoes pretty quickly! Instead, he lost his temper and yelled at his wife.

It is amazing to me that someone could jump up and down and sing, "Got any rivers you think are uncrossable" and then stumble over a pair of shoes!

What happened? That deacon didn't walk in love, and he didn't maintain the glow! God's will is that we maintain our fellowship with Him *every day*, speaking to ourselves in psalms, hymns, and spiritual songs and making melody in our hearts to the Lord (Eph. 5:18). That's not just talking about when we're in church. That's talking about an attitude of heart that we maintain wherever we are.

If you are filled with the Spirit, there will be a song in your heart whether you're at church, at home, or on the job — *wherever* you might be. That's a mark of a Spirit-filled life.

EPHESIANS 5:20
20 GIVING THANKS ALWAYS for all things unto God and the Father in the name of our Lord Jesus Christ.

Another mark of a Spirit-filled life is a heart full of thanksgiving to God no matter what circumstances you face.

1 THESSALONIANS 5:18
18 In every thing give thanks: for this is THE WILL OF GOD in Christ Jesus concerning you.

Some people think that when something bad happens to them, they're supposed to thank God *for* it. No, you don't thank God for what the devil has done. But right in the midst of tests and trials, you can give thanks to God because you know He's going to deliver you out of every test and trial. Giving thanks to God always — even in the midst of tests and trials — is God's will for your life.

The Bible says it's God's will for us to give *thanks* to Him, not grumble, gripe, and complain. If you murmur and complain about your circumstances, you'll be defeated because that means you're not in faith; you're over on the negative side of life. But if you'll give thanks to God and count your blessings, you'll get over on the positive side of life, and God can move on your behalf.

JAMES 1:2
2 My brethren, COUNT IT ALL JOY when ye fall
into divers temptations [different kinds of tests or
trials].

Notice James didn't say it *was* a joy when tests and trials come into our lives. He said *to count it* all joy. And if you *count it* all joy in the midst of tests and trials, you're going to start rejoicing with an attitude of thanksgiving to God.

I got ahold of this scripture as a young Baptist boy. I didn't know about the baptism in the Holy Ghost, but I had been healed and raised up from a deathbed. I was a young preacher, just starting out in the ministry, and I was going through a severe test of my faith.

I was visiting my grandfather's farm at the time, and I remember going to the barn to pray. Then I did exactly what this verse in James says: I *counted* it all joy. I knew I was standing on the Rock — on God's Word — so I looked the devil in the face and just started laughing.

Someone asked, "Did you *feel* like laughing?" No, I didn't *feel* like laughing. In fact, I felt like crying. But I started laughing in faith, because I knew in my heart that according to the Word, the victory was mine.

At that time, I had never seen anyone shout or jump or dance in the Holy Ghost. But while I was praising God behind my grandfather's barn, I did just that! I acted on James 1:2. I acted like God's Word is true, because it is. I rejoiced in faith, counting it all joy and counting the victory won.

While I was praising God behind Grandpa's barn, I said to the devil, "Just go ahead and put on all the pressure you can. But the tougher it gets, the more I'm going to shout and praise God." And I kept on praising God until the burden lifted, and the oppression of the enemy was gone.

Soon after that, my situation changed almost immediately for the better. But if I had stayed on the negative side and whined and complained about the test I was going through, I wouldn't have come through it victoriously. I wouldn't have experienced God's best in that particular circumstance.

You see, it's easy to laugh, shout, jump, and dance in a church service. But when you're really filled with the Holy Spirit, you're motivated by Him, and you're fervent in spirit and aglow with God all the time. And you can thank God in the midst of any and all circumstances.

If you're going through a test or trial, you're not thanking God *because* of the test. But you can thank Him because you have another opportunity to prove

Him faithful and to exercise and develop your faith. That's God's will for your life.

EPHESIANS 5:18,21,22
18 ... but be FILLED WITH THE SPIRIT. ...
21 SUBMITTING yourselves one to another in the fear of God.
22 Wives, SUBMIT yourselves unto your own husbands, as unto the Lord.

Another mark of a Spirit-filled life is humility. God wants us to have a brokenness or a meekness about us, not a harsh personality that makes us insist on having our own way all the time. Some people have a difficult time submitting to others. But when you're aglow with the Holy Spirit, it's easy.

Notice verse 22: *"Wives, submit yourselves unto your own husbands, as unto the Lord"* (Eph. 5:22). Paul uses the word "submit" in connection with husbands and wives, and he uses the same word in verse 21 in connection with believers submitting to one another.

Some people take Ephesians 5:22 out of its setting and try to make it say something it isn't really saying. For example, one fellow said to me, "Bless God, I'm the head of my home! And I told my wife, 'You're going to do what I tell you to do, or I'm going to knock your head off!'"

Does that sound like someone who's filled to overflowing with the Holy Spirit? No, that attitude is no more of God than I'm an astronaut!

A pastor once said to me, "I don't ever fast. I just can't do it. In fact, I drive home for lunch every day because I have to have three hot meals a day. And if I get home and my wife doesn't have a meal ready, there's hell to pay."

I thought to myself, *That fellow ought to get saved!* This pastor may have answered the call of God on his life, and he may have even been in the ministry God had called him to. But he wasn't wholeheartedly following the plan of God for his life because he wasn't fervent in spirit, and he wasn't walking in love.

I said before that maintaining a Spirit-filled life will affect every area of your life — spirit, soul, and body. On the other hand, *failing* to stay filled with the Spirit will affect you negatively in every area of your life too.

For example, this pastor didn't judge himself, and he died at a young age. That wasn't God's will for Him, but he didn't walk in the light of the Word, and he didn't judge himself. The Bible says, *"For if we would judge ourselves, we should not be judged"* (1 Cor. 11:31).

The Bible says wives are to submit to their husbands as unto the Lord (Eph. 5:22). It also says believers are to submit to *one another* (v. 21). Does that mean we're supposed to boss one another? No, and Ephesians 5:22 doesn't mean that a husband is supposed to boss his wife and act harshly toward her either.

God Wants Us To Be Teachable

The word "submit" simply means *to give in to one another.* That's hard to do sometimes from the natural standpoint. But if you're filled with the Spirit and you're maintaining the glow, it's easy, because a fervent spirit makes it easier to keep the flesh under the dominion of your spirit.

That's God's will for your life. And as you keep your flesh under subjection to your spirit, God's specific will and direction for your life will become clearer and clearer to you.

Some Christians fail to submit to one another, and they get easily offended. For example, some believers get offended at what a minister preaches or teaches from the Word.

Some folks get so offended they leave the church. But we need to submit to one another, and we need to submit to the Word! We need to maintain a *teachable* attitude.

Humility is a mark of the Spirit-filled life. And without humility and a teachable spirit, you will hinder yourself spiritually from fulfilling the plan of God for your life.

I have been in the ministry for more than fifty-five years, and it's amazing to me how many Christians who speak with tongues are unteachable.

They brag about the fact they spoke with tongues, and I'm glad they did speak with tongues. But too many of them stopped at the door, so to speak, when they should have come on in and walked with God.

We may not agree with each other on every little aspect of the Bible. But we can maintain a right atti-tude — a right spirit — toward each other, and we can

submit to one another. Of course, when folks get off doc-
trinally and get into error, we have to take a stand for
the truth in an attitude of love.

But we shouldn't argue over minor issues and minor
questions such as, "Is it a sin to drink lemonade?" That
may sound extreme, but folks have actually asked that.
Questions like that result in nothing more than doctri-
nal tangents. In other words, they don't affect a person's salvation in the least.

I said before that maintaining the glow is maintaining your spiritual life. And one way to maintain a
strong spiritual life full of the Holy Spirit is to maintain
a close fellowship with God through prayer.

> **ACTS 4:13-17,23,24,29-31**
> **13 Now when they** [the Sadducees] **SAW THE BOLD-**
> **NESS of Peter and John, and perceived that they**
> **were unlearned and ignorant men, they mar-**
> **velled; and they took knowledge of them, that they**
> **had been with Jesus.**
> **14 And beholding the man which was healed stand-**
> **ing with them, they could say nothing against it.**
> **15 But when they had commanded them to go**
> **aside out of the council, they conferred among**
> **themselves,**
> **16 Saying, What shall we do to these men? for that**
> **indeed a notable miracle hath been done by them**
> **is manifest to all them that dwell in Jerusalem;**
> **and we cannot deny it.**
> **17 BUT THAT IT SPREAD NO FURTHER AMONG**
> **THE PEOPLE, LET US STRAITLY THREATEN**
> **THEM, that they speak henceforth to no man in**
> **this name. . . .**
> **23 And being let go, they went to their own com-**

pany, and reported all that the chief priests and
elders had said unto them.
24 And when they heard that, they lifted up their
voice to God with one accord, and said. . . .
29 . . . Lord, behold their threatenings: and
GRANT UNTO THY SERVANTS, THAT WITH ALL
BOLDNESS they may speak thy word,
30 By stretching forth thine hand to heal; and
that signs and wonders may be done by the name
of thy holy child Jesus.
31 AND WHEN THEY HAD PRAYED, the place
was shaken where they were assembled together;
and THEY WERE ALL FILLED WITH THE HOLY
GHOST, and THEY SPAKE THE WORD OF GOD
WITH BOLDNESS.

This passage of Scripture is talking about the same
group of people who had received the gift of the Holy
Spirit in Acts 2 and began to speak in tongues as the
Spirit gave them utterance (Acts 2:4).

But notice Acts 4:31: *"And when they had prayed,
the place was shaken where they were assembled
together; and they were all FILLED WITH THE HOLY
GHOST, and they spake the word of God with boldness."* Those folks had already been filled with the Holy
Ghost in Acts 2, but God wanted them to *keep* being
filled.

Notice what happened in Acts 4 when the place was
shaken and they were all filled with the Holy Spirit. It
says, *". . . they spake the word of God with BOLD-
NESS"* (v. 31).

If you want to maintain a Spirit-filled life, maintain
a spirit of boldness through prayer. Then maintain

absolute obedience to God's Word and to His plan for your life — to what He's put in your heart to do.

Fulfilling God's Will Takes Obedience and Consecration

You will not fulfill the entire plan of God for your life all at once. Fulfilling God's plan for your life is a step-by-step journey of obedience and faithfulness to walk in the light of what you know He wants you to do each day. Obedience to God and His Word every day, even in the little things, will help you maintain a Spirit-filled life.

Also, if you want to maintain a Spirit-filled life, you must maintain an attitude of consecration to God.

If anything is lacking in Charismatic circles today, it's a lack of teaching on consecration and sanctification. Consecrating and sanctifying yourself to do the will of God is an ongoing process. In other words, you don't just consecrate yourself to do the will of God once and for all and then never think about it again.

You may not always know exactly what the Lord wants you to do in specific detail. But you should always be *willing* to do whatever He wants you to do and to go wherever He wants you to go. You will not be able to follow God's plan for your life unless you are *willing* to do whatever He might ask you to do.

In 1941 my wife and I prematurely left the Farmersville church as pastors. In other words, we left out of the will of God. For two years I itinerated in the field ministry, and then God sent us back to Farmersville to finish the spiritual work God had given us to do there.

While we were there the second time, we finished the job we should have done while we were there the first time. Finally, the time came when God told us to leave and go into the field ministry.

Later in my ministry, there was a period of time when I struggled with the thought of going back to the Farmersville church. Sometimes, even in the dead of winter, I would get out of bed at three or four o'clock in the morning and pray. I felt like God was dealing with me the third time about going back to that church.

"No, God," I would protest, "I don't want to go back there the third time, and that's a cinch."

Ordinarily, when I lay down at night to go to sleep, I would fall asleep the minute my head hit the pillow. But I struggled for weeks with the thought of going back to Farmersville, and I lost many a night's sleep over it.

Finally, I gave in and said, "All right, Lord. If You want me to go back to Farmersville, I'll go." When I said that, I heard the Lord just as plainly as if someone were physically present in the room. He said, "I don't want you to go back to Farmersville. I just want you to be *willing* to go."

I thought to myself, *Dear Lord, why did I fight that for so long? Think of all the hours I've prayed about not wanting to pastor that church. I could have saved myself so much anxiety if I'd just been willing to obey God in the first place!*

Then the Lord said something else to me that startled me, and it would do you well to pay careful attention to it too. He said, "Son, if you're not willing to go back to that church, then I can't use you in other areas where I want to use you."

If I hadn't been willing to go back to that church in Farmersville, God could not have used me as He is using me today. You see, you've got to be willing to do anything God wants you to do or He won't be able to use you at all.

Sometimes in following God's plan for your life, you'll have to do some things you'd rather not do. But if you will obey God step-by-step every day by walking in the light of His Word and being prayerful, obedient, and consecrated, you will stay aglow with His Spirit, and you'll eventually fulfill the plan of God for your life.

---

[1] Copyright 1945, Singspiration Music. Used by permission of Benson Music Group.

Chapter 3
Consecration to God's Plan

*Then cometh Jesus with them unto a place
called Gethsemane, and saith unto the disciples,
Sit ye here, while I go and pray yonder.*

*And he took with him Peter and the two sons
of Zebedee, and began to be sorrowful and very
heavy.*

*Then saith he unto them, My soul is exceed-
ing sorrowful, even unto death: tarry ye here,
and watch with me.*

*And he went a little farther, and fell on his
face, and prayed, saying, O my Father, if it be
possible, let this cup pass from me: nevertheless
NOT AS I WILL, BUT AS THOU WILT.*

*And he cometh unto the disciples, and find-
eth them asleep, and saith unto Peter, What,
could ye not watch with me one hour?*

*Watch and pray, that ye enter not into temp-
tation: the spirit indeed is willing, but the flesh
is weak.*

*He went away again the second time, and
prayed, saying, O my Father, if this cup may not
pass away from me, except I drink it, THY WILL
BE DONE.*

— Matthew 26:36-42

In this passage in Matthew 26, we can see the Lord Jesus Christ in His prayer life praying the prayer of dedication. These verses give us an example of Jesus' dedication as He consecrated Himself to do the Father's will. What was Jesus talking about when He prayed in the Garden of Gethsemane, "*. . . if it be possible, let this cup pass from me . . .*" (Matt. 26:39)?

Jesus knew the Cross lay before Him. He knew He was about to be made the sacrifice for sin on our behalf (Heb. 9:26).

Think of all the sins committed by mankind throughout the ages — all the immorality, debauchery, murder, and hatred! The Bible says Jesus was made sin for us, so that we might become the righteousness of God in Him (2 Cor. 5:21). But in the Garden of Gethsemane, knowing He was going to the Cross, the pure, spotless Son of God drew back from the prospect of bearing the sin of all mankind and experiencing separation from God.

No wonder when those final hours drew near, Jesus was sorrowful and heavy (Matt. 26:38; Mark 14:34). Even though Jesus knew His substitutionary death for mankind was the reason He had come into the world, He battled the temptation to draw back from what was to come, and He prayed to God, "If it be possible, let this cup pass from Me!"

As Jesus prayed in the Garden of Gethsemane, the Bible says He sweated as it were great drops of blood as He wrestled with the temptation to draw back from the Cross (Luke 22:44). It wasn't easy for Jesus to fulfill the Father's plan for Him. In fact, going to the Cross to be crucified for the sins of the world was a bitter cup to drink.

But Jesus knew the outcome of redemption would be the salvation of mankind, so for the joy set before Him, He surrendered to His Father's will (Heb. 12:2). Jesus prayed a prayer of consecration and dedication, saying, *". . . O my Father, if this cup may not pass away from me, except I drink it, THY WILL BE DONE"* (Matt. 26:42).

God is looking for believers who will dedicate and consecrate themselves wholly to Him to carry out *His* plan for their lives, just as Jesus did at Gethsemane and throughout His earthly ministry. The Lord's eyes roam throughout the earth to find people whose hearts are dedicated to Him (2 Chron. 16:9 *NIV*). God is looking for believers who will say as Jesus did, "Not *My* will, Father, but *Your* will be done."

Also, notice Jesus didn't just pray this prayer one time. He prayed virtually the same prayer three times (Matt. 26:39,42,44).

You see, the prayer of consecration is not a one-time prayer, as is the prayer of faith. The prayer of consecration is a prayer you pray throughout your life. You will only be able to follow God's plan for your life if you constantly maintain an attitude of consecration and surrender to the Lord's will, whatever it might be.

The Lack of Consecration in Believers

There seems to be a lack of deep consecration to do God's will among some Christians today. Recently, I was thinking about the difference between my experiences in Full Gospel circles fifty years ago and today. As I compared Full Gospel believers then and now, I realized there wasn't nearly as much sickness among Spirit-filled Christians fifty years ago as there is today.

I remembered the great manifestations of the Holy Spirit we used to experience in our meetings. The move of the Holy Ghost was also much greater and in more consistent demonstration back then than it is today. As I was thinking about this, the Spirit of God said to my spirit, "Yes, and the consecration of My people was greater too."

Let that soak in! Whether we choose to consecrate ourselves to obey God or choose not to obey God, it affects every other area of our lives as well!

I'm thoroughly convinced of the truth of what the Lord said to me. The consecration of believers *was* much deeper fifty years ago than it is today. Believers' appreciation and reverence for the things of God and the move of the Holy Spirit was much deeper too. And as a result, God honored that depth of consecration and reverence by giving His people great manifestations of the Holy Ghost.

Believers today need greater consecration and dedication to God. In the churches I pastored in the 1940s, we used to gather around the altar and pray at the end of nearly every service. We often sang the old hymn, "Is Your All on the Altar of Sacrifice Laid?"[1] We don't sing hymns like that much anymore, but many folks today need to heed the message of some of those old scriptural hymns.

It seems that many believers are willing to lay *some* things on the altar, but not *all*! But God's plan for their lives is hindered and many of His blessings are withheld because they haven't totally consecrated themselves to do God's will instead of their own.

Ministers need to teach about consecration so people's hearts will be stirred to surrender everything to God and to consecrate themselves wholly to follow God's plan for their lives.

Consider your own consecration to the Lord. Consider whether or not you are able to say from your heart, "Lord, I'll do whatever You ask me to do. I'll go anywhere You want me to go. And I'll stay where I am if You tell me to stay. No matter where You lead me, I'll carry the good news of Jesus Christ to others."

You see, you need to be willing to do *anything* God wants you to do. You need to commit yourself to obey God and do His will every day for the rest of your life.

Since I was first born again at the age of sixteen, I've understood the importance of total consecration to the Lord. I've been a Christian more than half a century, and I'm still praying the same prayer of consecration I prayed more than fifty years ago. I'm still praying, "Lord, I'll go where You want me to go. If You want me to go to Africa, I'll go. If You want me to stay where I am, I'll stay. I'll do what You want me to do."

Never Say 'Never'!

That doesn't mean I've never made a mistake in being completely dedicated to do what God wanted me to do. I remember once when I was a young pastor, I

attended a Bible convention. While talking with some of
the other pastors about a particular church, I made the
statement, "I'll tell you one thing! I would *never* pastor
that church."

Guess what I was doing less than two years later! I
was pastoring the very church I said I would never pastor!

I learned a good lesson from that experience. I
learned that the thing I'm unwilling to do could be the
very thing that God in His wisdom may need me to do.

You see, God's thoughts are higher than our
thoughts (Isa. 55:9). His ways are above our ways, and
He sees the whole picture. So it's a matter of trusting
God to know what is best for us.

After that experience, I determined never again to
say, "Lord, ask me to do anything but that. That's one
thing I'll *never* do." And I've endeavored to keep my
heart consecrated before God.

I remember one of our charter-class RHEMA gradu-
ates who learned that same lesson. Before he graduated, this man had told people he would never pastor.
And he went through the entire school year at RHEMA
convinced that God had called him to be an evangelist.

But at the charter-class graduation ceremony, when
I laid hands on this RHEMA student, I received a word
from the Lord for him. I began laughing in the Spirit,
saying, "You said you would never pastor. But you will!"

Then I laid hands on his wife and once again started
laughing in the Spirit. I said to her by the unction of
the Holy Spirit, "And you said you would never be a

pastor's wife. But you will be, and you'll be so contented and glad that you are!"

Soon after graduation, this man was driving down a country road, praying about the Lord's next step for him. And the Spirit of God said to him, "Go home right now. Within thirty minutes, a man will call you and ask you to come and pastor a church in a small town in Oklahoma. I want you to accept that pastorate."

The man immediately drove home. Soon after he arrived home, the phone rang. Just as the Lord had said, the man on the phone asked this RHEMA graduate to come and pastor the church in that small town. The RHEMA graduate obeyed God and accepted the offer.

This man and his wife began pastoring, and they were blessed for their obedience. They found that they were contented and full of joy as they obeyed God's will, even though it meant doing what they said they would never do!

Be Willing To Do Anything for God

It's so important for you to be willing to do anything God tells you to do. Unwillingness to obey God can hinder or delay His plan from being fulfilled in your life. The truth of that statement can be seen in a testimony I once heard about a nationally known Full Gospel evangelist.

This evangelist related that he had been born again and filled with the Holy Spirit when he was thirteen years old. At that time, he also sensed a call to the ministry on his life. However, the evangelist explained that as a new Christian, he was afraid God might tell him to go to China if he answered the call to the ministry. In his natural mind, he decided that China was one place he didn't want to go.

For many years this young man struggled with the prospect of God's sending him to China. He avoided drawing close to God because he didn't want to hear what God might tell him. Therefore, he kept himself from developing spiritually, and he wandered backslidden and out of God's will for years because there was one thing he wasn't willing to do — and that was to go to China as a missionary.

Several times during those years of running away from God, this young man would go to church, come forward to pray at the altar, and temporarily surrender to God again.

You see, a person can temporarily surrender to the Lord. At the time he prays, he may really mean it. But the real test comes when he gets up from the altar and is required to obey God and do something he doesn't want to do. If it was only a superficial surrender to the Lord, the person will draw back from the commitment he just made and go on doing what *he* wants to do in life.

One night at a revival meeting when this young man was almost thirty years old, he once again went to the altar to recommit his life to God. This time he was serious about serving the Lord, no matter what sacrifice it might mean.

Relating what had happened to him as a young man, this evangelist said, "As soon as I got back into fellowship with God, I was faced once again with the question of whether or not I would answer God's call to the ministry."

You see, that divine call had been on the young man's life all those years he had been running from God, because the gifts and calling of God are without repentance (Rom. 11:29). God was just waiting for him to surrender his life completely to Him.

The evangelist continued: "This time I just threw up my hands and cried, 'All right, Lord, I surrender! I'll go to China if You want me to! Wherever You want me to go, I'll go. Not my will, but *Yours* be done.'

"Immediately, so loudly I thought everyone else in the room must have heard it, I heard the Lord say, 'I don't want you to go to China. I just want you to be *willing* to go.'"

Once this man fully surrendered to God, he became one of the leading evangelists in this nation. But, you see, he couldn't have been the evangelist God had called him to be in the United States unless he was willing to be an evangelist *anywhere* God told him to go, even China.

The same is true in each of our lives. We will only experience the fullness of God's plan and the full measure of His anointing and blessing on our lives if we are willing to obey Him in every area of our lives.

You see, God wants us *fully* surrendered to His will. He knows if we're not willing to obey Him in one area, that unwillingness will carry over into other areas of our lives and will hinder us from running the race He has set before us.

Nearly everything I'm doing today, my natural mind didn't want to do when God first talked to me about it. At one time, I didn't even want to preach!

Before I was saved when I was a young boy, I wanted to be a lawyer. And if you've ever noticed, in my preaching and teaching, I often "argue my case" in much the way a lawyer would, only I prove my case with the Scriptures. I don't try to do that; it's just a part of my personality.

When I was nine or ten years old, I would often go to the town courthouse because I loved to sit up in the balcony and listen to the lawyers as they argued their cases. And as I listened to them, I was just sure I could have done a better job than some of them!

But then I was born again on April 22, 1933, at twenty minutes to eight o'clock in the south bedroom of 405 North College Street in McKinney, Texas, while lying paralyzed on a deathbed with an incurable blood disease and a deformed heart. And the first thing I said was, "Lord, You get me up from this bed of sickness, and I'll go preach."

That was another way of saying, "Not my will, Lord, but Thy will be done." It was my way as a teenager of praying the prayer of surrender and consecration. Sixteen months later, the Lord raised me up supernaturally as I prayed the prayer of faith. And I've been preaching ever since!

I've prayed the prayer of consecration countless times since then. For instance, while I was pastoring my last church in Van, Texas, the Lord began dealing with me about a change coming in my ministry that would take me out of the pastoral ministry and into the field ministry.

For several years I had sensed in my spirit that this change was coming. God was preparing me for the next stage in my ministry.

At this point in our lives, my family and I were living more comfortably than we had ever been in all the previous years of my ministry. I was making more money than I had ever made in my life. We were living in the best parsonage we had ever lived in. I was driving the best automobile I had ever driven, and we were wearing the best clothes we had ever worn since I'd started in the ministry.

Not only that, but the people in the church were pleased with me as the pastor. The board members in the church once told me, "Brother Hagin, we'd be glad if you stayed here and pastored forever."

It would have been fine with me if God had told me to continue pastoring that little church indefinitely. I wasn't dealing with any major problems in the church, our congregation was growing, and there were times to relax and enjoy fellowship with family and friends.

But then the Lord began dealing with me about going out into the field ministry. That was a cup I didn't want to drink! I had a wife and two children to support, and I didn't want to leave the security of pastoring. I had pastored twelve of my fifteen years of ministry. For me, going out into field ministry was a big step of faith into the unknown.

I want you to know that I prayed more than once, asking the Lord to let that cup pass from me. I spent two years praying about it! I talked to God every day about it.

Several times I prayed all night long about it. When the sun rose at dawn, I would still be walking up and down the aisles of the sanctuary, talking to God about pastoring instead of going out into field ministry.

I would tell God, "Lord, everyone is pleased with me as the pastor. My family and I are enjoying life here. Everything is fine." In so many words, I was telling God, "Lord, why don't You leave well enough alone? Don't disturb my comfortable life here."

But I just couldn't get God to change His mind! You see, the Bible says, ". . . *the gifts and calling of God are without repentance*" (Rom. 11:29). So I finally surrendered to God's will and told Him, "Not my will, Father, but Yours be done," and in 1949 I took a major step of faith and went into the field ministry.

When I first started out in the field ministry, I didn't know how good the results of drinking that cup of obedience would be! Yes, there were hard places to endure, and it was tough going for a while. But over the years God has blessed us beyond anything we could ever have imagined, because we were obedient to *His* plan, not to our own desires.

We have all had to drink some cups in life we would rather have passed up. But when we know that the cup is the Lord's will for us, we can rest assured the outcome will be for our good and to God's glory. That's why we need to stay open to God's will and pray just as Jesus did, "Not my will, Father, but *Yours* be done."

Many Christians have never surrendered everything to the Lord. They are willing to make Jesus Lord of *part* of their lives. But sometimes they aren't willing to give up control of certain areas that their carnal nature holds dear. Some believers profess they've laid everything on the altar, but in reality they are holding back a part of themselves from the Lord.

It's so important to make a quality decision once and for all to go all out for God and follow His plan for your life. That decision will be an anchor to your soul to keep you in God's perfect will when the devil tries to bring his best temptations into your life to distract and deter you from the plan of God.

You see, the devil will bid high for you — he'll use his *best* temptations to try to keep you from obeying God. If you've never fully surrendered everything to the Lord, you stand in danger of being persuaded by the devil's temptations to pursue your own will and fleshly inclinations and desires and lose out on God's best for you.

The Crossroad of Decision

Many Christians are at a crossroad in their lives right now. In other words, they face decisions that will affect the course of their lives. They are at a crossroad where they must decide if they are going to consecrate themselves fully to do God's will, no matter what He asks them to do.

Believers who stand at a crossroad can choose to follow the path of their own plans and desires. That path may look wide and bright and stretch straight before them as far as their eyes can see.

But if they continue to lean to their own understanding and disobey God, that straight, wide path will eventually lead them into darkness. In other words, believers who don't choose the perfect will of God will encounter trials in life God never intended them to encounter.

On the other hand, the path God has planned for obedient believers may be a narrow one that goes over mountains and through deep valleys. God's path might have bends and curves in it that sometimes obscure their view.

Believers who follow God's way may not always be able to see very far down the path, because following God is a step-by-step walk of faith and obedience. But despite the difficulties that lie on the path of obedience, such a great future in the Lord awaits those who choose to walk in God's ways!

You might say, "No, I don't much believe I want to take that narrow, curving path where I can't see what's up ahead! I don't know where it's going. I can see the other path stretched out wide and straight before me. But if I go down that narrow road of God's choosing, I can't see beyond the mountains. That way of obedience looks rugged and difficult."

But the road of obedience is the one you must choose if you want to follow God's plan for your life. And as you choose to obey God, He will furnish you with the power and ability to climb over the mountains you are facing right now, as well as the mountains up ahead that you can't see yet.

Your path will grow brighter and brighter, and many other lives will be influenced for Jesus because of your obedience. For, you see, it is on the path of obedience where God reveals His glory and your strength is renewed day by day. And when you finish your course and meet Jesus face to face, how glad you will be that you obeyed God!

Each of us will experience many crossroads in our lives — some more crucial than others. At each crossroad, we must renew our commitment to do the Lord's will, not our own.

That's why we must pray the prayer of consecration over and over in our walk with the Lord and dedicate ourselves to fully obey Him and His Word.

Consecrate yourself wholly unto the Lord. Even though in your natural mind you want to follow your own plans and desires, consider yourself dead to carnal inclinations.

And although it may seem difficult at times to say no to your own will and plans, the end result of obedience will cause your spirit to rejoice. You will make your way prosperous, and you will be fulfilled beyond anything your natural mind can imagine.

There is simply no comparison between a life that's lived by walking in the flesh and one lived according to God's perfect plan!

Pray this prayer of commitment to God from your heart:

Lord, I present myself unto You. May Your will be done in my life. May I never forget that I have surrendered all I am to You.

I commit myself to be one whom You can use — consecrated and separated unto Your purposes. I'll pay the price by denying the flesh. If You call me in the nighttime, I'll get on my knees and pray. If I am never seen of men, and if I always work behind the scenes, still I will be faithful.

I lay aside all personal ambition. I'll be one who walks in the Spirit and in Your perfect will. In Jesus' Name, Your will *shall* be wrought in my heart, in my life, and in my ministry.

When you are worshipping the Lord with other believers and the Presence of the Holy Spirit is in manifestation, it's easy to say those words and to dedicate your life to the Lord.

But in the hour of test and trial, when circumstances seem to toss you this way and that, hold fast to that same dedication. Maintain that same determination of mind, will, and purpose and say with assurance, "I *will* walk with the Father. I *will* let Him work out His purpose in my life."

By staying consecrated even when it's difficult to do so, you will have learned the great lesson of obedience and consecration and faith. And as you daily choose to obey God's will and run the race He has set before *you*, you will be a blessing to many. And God will lead you to a wide, open place — a place of abundance in every area of your life!

---

[1] "Is Your All on the Altar of Sacrifice Laid?" by Elisha Hoffman.

Chapter 4
Learning To Be Led
By the Holy Spirit

For as many as are led by the Spirit of God,
they are the sons of God.

— Romans 8:14

Every child of God can learn how to be led by the
Holy Spirit. God's richest blessings await those who follow after His Spirit, instead of being directed only by
their senses and circumstances. But in order to be
Spirit-led, you will have to consecrate yourself to God's
plan for your life instead of following after a plan of
your own making.

Learning to be led by the Holy Spirit is of primary
importance if you are going to obey God. If you can't
discern what the Lord is saying to your spirit, you'll
have a difficult time following His plan and purpose for
your life. It's that simple.

God Leads You by Your Spirit

How can we discern the Lord's leading and learn to
cooperate with Him so we can follow His plan for our
lives?[1] First of all, we must understand that God con-

63

tacts us and deals with us through our *spirit*.

You see, God is *not* a physical being, so He doesn't respond to the call of our *fleshly nature*. And He is not a mind, so He doesn't respond to the call of our *intellect* or our *emotions*.

That's where so many folks miss it. They try to reach God through their mind and feelings. They say, "Oh, if I could only *feel* God's Presence when I pray!"

But what they actually need to do is crucify their flesh, renew their mind with God's Word, and get quiet on the inside as they seek the Lord in prayer (Gal. 5:24; Rom. 12:2). Then the Holy Spirit would respond unto the cry of their *spirit*.

God is a Spirit, a divine Personality (John 4:24). Man is also a spirit being. Man *is* a spirit, he *has* a soul (which includes the mind, will, and emotions), and he *lives in* a body (*see* Gen. 1:26,27; 2 Cor. 5:1-4; 1 Thess. 5:23; Heb. 4:12).

The spirit man or inward man is the eternal part of a person that gives the outward man color and personality. And it is the inward man of a believer — his spirit — that hears what the Spirit of God is saying.

The Bible says, *"The SPIRIT OF MAN is the candle of the Lord, searching all the inward parts of the belly"* (Prov. 20:27). The Bible also says the Holy Spirit bears witness with our *spirit* (Rom. 8:16).

In other words, the Holy Spirit will use our spirit to

guide and enlighten us as to God's will for our lives. He doesn't communicate with us directly through our *mind* or our *body*, because He dwells in our *spirit*. Therefore, He communicates with us through our spirit.

We can expect the Holy Spirit to guide and direct us so we can fulfill God's plan and purpose for our lives. The Bible tells us that ". . . *as many as are led by the Spirit of God, they are the sons of God"* (Rom. 8:14). Notice it does *not* say, "As many as are led by the *mind* or *flesh*, they are the sons of God."

And that verse also doesn't say, "As many as are led by *prophets* or by *someone else telling them what to do*, they are the sons of God." Although it's good at times to seek wise counsel from someone you respect spiritually, you shouldn't look to man to receive God's guidance for you. That's unscriptural.

As Christians, we all have the Spirit of God, and we are each responsible to discern the Lord's leading for ourselves. We are to be led by the Holy Spirit according to God's Word, *not* by other people's guidance or opinions.

How does the Holy Spirit lead us? The first and foremost way God leads His children is by *the inward witness*. Romans 8:16 talks about the inward witness: *"The Spirit itself* [Himself] *BEARETH WITNESS with OUR SPIRIT, that we are the children of God."*

When you are born again, the Holy Spirit lets you know you are a child of God *by bearing witness with your spirit.*

You don't know you're a child of God because some-one prophesied to you that you're saved. And you don't know you're born again because someone told you, "In my opinion, you're a Christian."

No, you know you're a child of God because God's Spirit bears witness with your spirit that you are born again. You might not be able to explain to someone else *how* you know you're saved, but you just know it down on the inside. You know you've become a new creature in Christ (Rom. 10:9,10; 2 Cor. 5:17).

The inward witness is the way the Holy Spirit guides you in the most important event that could ever happen to you — becoming a child of God. Therefore, it's logical that the inward witness will be the primary way the Holy Spirit will continue to guide you through-out your Christian walk.

In my own life and ministry, I'm almost always led by the inward witness. Yes, at times I've had spectacu-lar guidance, such as visions, but most of the time I'm led by the inward witness. That's the number one way God leads all of His children.

As you seek to follow God's plan for your life, there will be many times your spirit will know things by the inward witness that your head doesn't know. Your spirit will pick up that information from the Spirit of God who dwells within.

Sometimes it can be difficult to explain to another person in logical terms how you know something by the inward witness of the Holy Spirit. You just know it on the inside. It's not a physical feeling. It's a *spiritual sense* or *perception.*

For instance, when Paul was a prisoner on board a ship headed for Rome, he said, ". . . *Sirs, I PERCEIVE that this voyage will be with hurt and much damage, not only of the lading and ship, but also of our lives"* (Acts 27:10).

Paul didn't say, "The Holy Ghost spoke to me" or "I had a vision." He said, "I *perceive* that this voyage will be fraught with danger." Evidently Paul had an inward witness or a spiritual perception about the voyage. His spirit picked up that knowledge from the Holy Spirit dwelling within him.

The second way the Holy Spirit leads us is through *the inward voice,* also called *the still small voice.* Did you know your inward man has a voice, just like your outward man does? The voice of your spirit is called your *conscience.*

You don't hear the inward voice — the voice of your inward man — with your physical ears, like you do the voice of your outward man. You hear the voice of your inward man on the inside of you in your spirit. Your spirit man will speak to you by the still small voice of your conscience and pass on to your mind the information he receives from the Holy Spirit within.

The third way the Holy Spirit leads you is through *the authoritative Voice of the Holy Spirit.* Although the

Holy Spirit may choose to speak to the believer in the authoritative Voice, we are not to seek after voices. These things happen as the Holy Spirit wills (1 Cor. 12:11).

There is a distinct difference between the inward voice of your own spirit and the audible Voice of the Holy Spirit. When the Holy Spirit speaks to you, it is more authoritative.

You'll hear the authoritative Voice of the Holy Spirit on the inside, in your inward man. Or you might hear His Voice out loud; it can seem just as real to you as if you are hearing a person speak to you out loud.

You see, when the Holy Spirit speaks to you, it can actually seem *audible*, even though no one else in the same room hears it. That's because the Holy Spirit doesn't speak in the *sense realm*, since He doesn't have a physical body. He is a Spirit, a divine Personality, and He speaks in the *spirit realm*.

You are also a spirit being. So when you hear the Holy Spirit speak, you are hearing His Voice with your spirit. And His Voice *is* audible in the spirit realm.

Spiritual things are just as real as material things. In fact, the spiritual realm is even more real than the natural realm because God, who is a Spirit, *created* the material, natural realm. So if you are going to successfully follow God's plan for your life, you need to become more Spirit-conscious than you are mind-conscious or body-conscious.

Too many Christians spend their whole lives conscious only of what their natural senses tell them. They are sense-conscious and body-ruled, and because of that, they often become spiritually deaf.

Their spiritual ears get stopped up, so to speak, because they don't pay attention to the Holy Spirit inside them, and their heart is all cluttered up with natural concerns.

Other Christians don't ever hear from God because *they* are the ones doing all the talking. They chatter all the time, and they don't take time to listen to what the Lord is trying to tell them in their spirit.

And some Christians don't even know they *have* spiritual ears or that they are *supposed* to be hearing anything from the Holy Spirit!

Develop Your Spirit So You Can Know God's Will

Too often our problem in following God's plan for our lives is that we have failed to train our spirit as we should have. We have spent most of our lives in the mental and physical realms, developing our intellect at the expense of our heart.

When we neglect the development of our spirit, our intellect takes the throne in our lives. And our spirit, the part of us which should dominate and guide our mind and body, is kept locked away in prison, so to speak, and is not permitted to function.

But the Holy Spirit through the inward witness is always seeking to give guidance to our mind — if we would only take time to develop our spirit and to listen.

Here's an important point to remember if you are ever going to develop your spirit. You must determine to *always keep a tender conscience.*

Don't violate your conscience. Instead, make it a practice to always instantly obey your spirit. Remember, your conscience is the voice of your spirit, and it relates to your mind what the Spirit of God is saying to you in your heart.

If you persist in violating your conscience, you will make your conscience calloused to the Holy Spirit's promptings. Spiritual things will become indistinct to you, and your conscience will no longer be a safe guide. Once your conscience is seared, it will be difficult for you to discern the Lord's leading and to follow His plan.

Also, as you seek to develop your spirit, remember to *make sure you aren't being led by your flesh.* This is where many Christians miss it. They make decisions according to their own fleshly nature, desires, and inclinations.

And because their spirits are not in tune to the Holy Spirit inside them, they miss the things of the Spirit which God has prepared for them in their spiritual race.

It will also hinder the development of your spirit if you *allow yourself to be led by your soul — your feelings, natural reasonings, and emotions.*

ⓧ fear
ⓧ soul
ⓧ emotion
ⓧ outward circumstances

This is another area where Christians often miss it. They allow themselves to get emotionally worked up about plans and desires of their own making, and then they convince themselves that it is the Lord leading them. But actually, they are being led by their emotions, not their spirit, and their emotions lead them astray.

It's also important in the development of your spirit *not to be led by outward circumstances.*

When I was a young pastor, I knew pastors who were led by circumstances. When they encountered problems in their church, they'd say things like, "If I ever get the Sunday school attendance back up to where it was, I'm going to leave."

Or they'd say, "Once the finances of the church are doing better, I'm going to take another pastorate." But, you see, those pastors were being led by natural circumstances rather than by the Holy Spirit.

As a pastor, I never let circumstances move me. It didn't bother me the least bit if the Sunday school attendance or the offerings fell off. I never allowed myself to be motivated by crowds or money or any other natural circumstance.

When I encountered problems in the churches I pastored, I'd just say to myself: "I don't ascertain the will of God by outward circumstances. I ascertain the will of God by what He's saying to me in my spirit. God told me to pastor this church, and I'm not going to question

His judgment. I'm not going to wonder whether or not He'll tell me to leave next week or next month. That isn't any of my business; that's *His* business. I'm going to stay put until He tells me to go.

"If God wants me to go somewhere else, He has enough sense to talk to me. He's an intelligent Being, and so am I. I'll understand what He's saying to me. I'm in contact with God, and I'm open to His leading. He'll give me the signal when He's ready for me to move on. I'll know it on the inside of me by the inward witness."

That's how I've operated in my almost sixty years of ministry as I've followed God's plan for my life. I go as much by what the Lord *doesn't* say as I do by what He *does* say.

In other words, I live by the principles of God's Word and by the leading of the Holy Spirit in my spirit. I just keep heading in the direction the Lord has already told me to go unless He sees fit to initiate a new direction in His plan for my life and ministry. I don't try to initiate a new direction on my own.

In developing your spirit and ascertaining God's direction for your life, it will also help you to *strive for unity and agreement with those around you who are spiritually mature.* Be careful about making a move when those who are close to you and whom you respect spiritually are not in agreement that you have the leading of the Lord.

For instance, the Early Church practiced biblical

principles of unity and agreement in making some decisions, especially regarding ministry. We see an example of that in Acts 13 when Paul and Barnabas were being set apart for the ministry.

ACTS 13:1-3
1 Now there were in the church that was at Antioch CERTAIN PROPHETS AND TEACHERS; as Barnabas, and Simeon that was called Niger, and Lucius of Cyrene, and Manaen, which had been brought up with Herod the tetrarch, and Saul.
2 As THEY ministered to the Lord, and fasted, the Holy Ghost said, Separate me Barnabas and Saul [Paul] for the work whereunto I have called them.
3 And when THEY had fasted and prayed, and laid their hands on them, THEY sent them away.

The Bible doesn't say *how* the Holy Spirit spoke in this instance. One of the prophets could have spoken out by the unction of the Holy Ghost in prophecy. Or someone could have heard the authoritative Voice of the Holy Spirit.

But it doesn't really matter how the Holy Spirit spoke. The point is that all five ministers involved in that meeting at Antioch were in agreement that it was the leading of the Lord to separate Barnabas and Paul to the work of the ministry.

Now it's true that as you follow God's plan for your life, you're going to have to make some decisions for yourself. You don't need to always be questioning everyone around you about what they think your decision should be. God may not tell others what He wants you to do in a given situation.

Too many Christians let others tell them what to do because they don't want to take the responsibility of seeking God for guidance themselves. But every believer has the responsibility of receiving the Lord's direction for his own life.

On the other hand, we read in Acts 13 that everyone involved agreed on what the leading of the Lord was and then acted on it.

Therefore, it is certainly scriptural for those whom you trust spiritually to be in agreement when you're making a major decision that will greatly affect your life. But that doesn't mean you're supposed to allow others to take the responsibility for receiving guidance for your life.

However, many times it's wise to consider the counsel of those who know the Lord and who care about you. In my own life, I can think of some people whose spiritual walk I have the utmost confidence in. And there are times when I talk to them about decisions I need to make. The Bible says, *"Where no counsel is, the people fall: but in the multitude of counsellors there is safety"* (Prov. 11:14).

Also, it's important that those whose lives are affected by your decision agree that the Lord is leading in that particular direction. For instance, in the early 1940s when the Lord began dealing with me about going back to pastor the church in Farmersville (I had left the church earlier out of God's will), I wanted that decision to be confirmed by my wife.

I was pastoring another church at the time, and I had been struggling with the prospect of going back to the Farmersville church for about a month.

Sometimes I'd be praying in the sanctuary, and the burden for the Farmersville church would come on me so strongly that I'd get up and physically run out of the building. I was trying to run away from that burden. I kept telling the Lord, "I don't want to go back there and pastor!"

You know, sometimes your flesh and your mind rebel against what the Lord is asking you to do. And you can get all mixed up if you try to listen to your physical senses, your mind, *and* your spirit.

So finally I prayed, "Lord, if you want us to go back to Farmersville, bear witness to that fact with my wife too."

Soon after that, Oretha and I were washing dishes together, and I asked her, "Honey, has the Lord been talking to you about anything?"

"No, not that I know of," she answered.

"Well, let me know if He does tell you anything," I said to her.

I waited about thirty days, and one morning when we were washing dishes together again, I asked my wife, "Have you heard anything from the Lord?"

Oretha said, "No, I haven't." Sometimes people have heard from the Lord, but they don't recognize it as the Lord's leading.

So I asked her, "Do you have any leading to resign from this church and go pastor another church?"

"No," she said.

"Do you have anything in your heart at all about the church in Farmersville?" I asked.

"Oh," she said, "I thought that was just me." You see, she had something from the Lord and just didn't recognize it.

"Well, let me ask you a question," I said. "Do you want to go back to Farmersville to pastor?"

"Oh, no!" she exclaimed. "A thousand times no!"

I said, "Well, then, it couldn't be you, could it? *You* don't want to go back there."

"I guess you're right," she answered.

In the natural, neither one of us wanted to go back to that church. But we both obeyed God and went, and we were happier pastoring that church than we had ever been in our lives.

Because we had left that church prematurely the first time, God wasn't able to accomplish what He wanted to. But as a result of our obedience to go back there, God was able to teach me how to develop that congregation spiritually more than any other church we ever pastored.

We learned many valuable lessons there. God's way is always best! But the point I'm trying to get across to you is that the Lord dealt with both of us by the inward witness to go back to that church in Farmersville.

Oretha and I both agreed that the Lord was leading us in that direction. Whenever possible, that's the way it should be when more than one person is going to be affected by a decision.

There may be times when others don't agree with the direction you sense the Lord is leading you to take. Ultimately, you have to follow the Lord's leading to the best of your ability. But when others aren't in agreement with you, be very careful to make sure it's the Lord's leading.

Get God's Direction Clear in Your Spirit Before You Act

It's important not to be too quick when making decisions that affect your life. Remember what Jesus told me: "I'd rather you be too slow than too fast."

Therefore, if you're going to develop your spirit so you can discern God's plan for your life, you need to *take enough time to pray until you have the Lord's direction clear in your spirit.*

The trouble with some Christians is that when they do receive some direction about God's plan for their lives, they mix that revelation with their own feelings

and thinking. They follow after their own human thinking and entirely miss *God's* thinking on the matter.
Then the plan doesn't turn out right, and they get confused, wondering if they ever really heard from God.

The only way you can keep that from happening is
to get in the Presence of God long enough to sift out
your own human emotions and thoughts and lay them
on the altar before God. Then pray and meditate on the
Word until you hear from the Lord in your spirit and
you know on the inside what to do.

What you need to realize is that God's thoughts are
so much higher than man's thoughts (Isa. 55:9). And it
is in God's Word where you find His thoughts. That's
why meditating and feeding constantly on God's Word
renews your mind so your mind can come into agreement with your spirit.

You see, the voice that speaks to you in the Word is
the same voice that leads you by your spirit. So being in
the Word sharpens your spiritual perception and ability
to hear God's voice in your own spirit.

Therefore, waiting before the Lord in prayer *and* in
the Word is vitally important if you want to walk in
God's ways according to *His* thinking, rather than
according to your own natural reasoning.

When I was still young in my Christian walk, I
learned to take time to wait before the Lord in prayer
and in the Word until I got it clear in my spirit what He
wanted me to do. Sometimes I've sought God in prayer

for several days about His direction. In fact, I have
sometimes prayed several months before making major
decisions in my ministry.

I don't mean I was on my knees praying all the
time. I still went about my daily business. But whenever I could, I'd pray, many times all night long. Much
of the time I'd pray in other tongues.

Actually, one of the greatest assets God has provided for the believer in seeking God's plan for his life is
the baptism of the Holy Spirit with the evidence of
speaking in other tongues (Acts 2:2-4).[2]

The Bible says that when you pray in an unknown
tongue, your *spirit* prays (1 Cor. 14:14). Your spirit is
actively communicating with God when you pray in
other tongues as the Spirit gives you utterance. This is
a great enablement in prayer because it is through your
spirit that God gives you guidance.

First Corinthians 14:2 says that when you pray in
tongues, you are speaking mysteries to God. So as you
seek the Lord for guidance and direction, the Holy
Spirit will help you pray out the mysteries of God's plan
for your life as you pray in other tongues.

In my own Christian experience, I've found that
praying in other tongues is one of the best ways to get
my body quiet and my mind in neutral so I can hear
what my *spirit* is saying. You see, you can be just as
noisy with your mind as you can be with your hands
and feet! And if your mind is hollering at you — con-

stantly bombarding you with its soulish thoughts or the devil's lies — you aren't going to hear what the Holy Spirit is saying to your spirit.

Over the years, it has become easier for me to get my mind and body quiet as I pray. It used to take me at least an hour and a half of praying in tongues to get my soul and my body quiet. But now it only takes me a few minutes.

You see, spiritual things have to be practiced just like natural things do. For instance, baseball players practice in the spring in order to get ready for the upcoming baseball season. Similarly, the more you wait before the Lord and pray in other tongues, the easier it will be to get quiet and listen to your heart.

Of course, that's not easy on the flesh. Your body won't necessarily want to pray. It's a whole lot easier to watch television or to visit Susie Q or Joe Blow down the street than it is to make yourself pray, isn't it? But if you are going to receive God's wisdom and direction in your life, you'll have to keep your body under subjection to your spirit and diligently give yourself to prayer (1 Cor. 9:27; 1 Peter 4:7).

As I sought God's guidance about various decisions, sometimes I'd pray night after night over a period of several weeks. I wouldn't stop until I got it clear in my spirit what the Lord wanted me to do.

The whole time I'd be praying, I'd have my "spiritual antenna" up. Do you know what I mean by that? In other words, I was constantly alert in my spirit to hear what God was saying to me.

You, too, can put up your spiritual antenna simply by an act of faith. On the inside of you, reach toward God with your spirit. As you do, you will contact the Father God, who is a Spirit, and He will respond to your spirit.

As I prayed during those prolonged seasons of prayer, from somewhere deep inside, the knowledge of what God wanted me to do would rise up in me. The Lord's wisdom and guidance would take shape and form within me, and eventually I'd know on the inside of me exactly what direction I was supposed to take. Once I got it clear in my spirit, no one could knock the knowledge of God's plan out of me. I had it!

Getting God's direction clear in your spirit is what will carry you through to victory when the trials come. If you don't know for sure what God's will is for you concerning a particular matter, you could be easily swayed by adverse and contrary circumstances. If you don't have God's direction clear in your spirit and you make a decision anyway, you could waste a lot of time wavering back and forth in fear wondering if you missed God.

Without the knowledge of God's will fixed firmly in your spirit, you'll ride the waves of circumstances, so to speak, up one day and down the next. And you'll eventually get off course, because you'll be led by natural circumstances rather than by the leading of the Holy Spirit in your spirit. *Knowing* God's will in your spirit is your anchor to keep you on course no matter what comes against you.

Rid Your Heart of Any Hindrances

So make it your lifelong aim to develop your spirit and to always get God's guidance and direction clear in your spirit before you make a move. However, remember this: You won't be able to accomplish that goal unless you *get rid of anything in your heart that might be a hindrance to your prayer life.* If you don't rid your heart of hindrances, you'll spend a lot of time praying with no results.

What can hinder your prayer life? Jesus gives us one hindrance in Mark 11:25. After talking about the prayer of faith in Mark 11:24, Jesus states that unforgiveness is a hindrance to getting prayers answered.

> **MARK 11:24-26**
> **24 Therefore I say unto you, What things soever ye desire, when ye pray, believe that ye receive them, and ye shall have them.**
> **25 And WHEN YE STAND PRAYING, FORGIVE, if ye have ought against any: that your Father also which is in heaven may forgive you your trespasses.**
> **26 But if ye do not forgive, neither will your Father which is in heaven forgive your trespasses.**

When you pray — forgive. Why did Jesus say that? Because Jesus knew our prayers would be ineffectual if we harbor unforgiveness in our hearts toward anyone.

Unless you practice walking in the love of God and you are quick to forgive, you will greatly hinder the development of your spirit and your ability to receive guidance and direction from the Lord — *because it's by your heart or spirit that He leads you.*

The Book of First Peter mentions another hindrance to the believer's prayer life.

> **1 PETER 3:7-9**
> **7 Likewise, ye husbands, dwell with them [your** wives] **according to knowledge, giving honour unto the wife, as unto the weaker vessel, and as being heirs together of the grace of life; THAT YOUR PRAYERS BE NOT HINDERED.**
> **8 Finally, be ye all of one mind, having compassion one of another, love as brethren, be pitiful, be courteous:**
> **9 Not rendering evil for evil, or railing for railing: but contrariwise blessing; knowing that ye are thereunto called, that ye should inherit a blessing.**

Verse 7 says that husbands can hinder their prayers by not giving honor to their wife as a fellow heir of the grace of life. The truth is, both husbands and wives can hinder their prayer lives and their spiritual development by not walking in love toward each other. That's absolutely the truth!

That scriptural principle is also true for every believer. In other words, if you don't rid your heart of every bit of animosity, ill will, or unforgiveness, you are *blocking* the channel of communication between you and God.

These are not the only hindrances to your prayer life and to the development of your spirit so you can successfully follow God in life.

Your prayer life will be hindered if you don't strip off everything that is a bondage to you personally — every weight and sin that would try to hold you back from running your spiritual race to the best of your ability (Heb. 12:1).

So don't dam up the flood tide of God's blessing and glory and guidance! Don't hold on to weights and sins that clog the flow of His Spirit in your life. Get those things out of your mind and your heart. Repent of them and get them under the blood of Jesus.

Take care of any hindrance to your prayer life *before* you begin to seek God for guidance on a matter. Then you can be assured that your heart is clear and uncluttered so you can hear what the Holy Spirit is saying to you.

Let God Remove the Obstacles In Your Path

Once you do have God's guidance on a matter, don't be concerned with seemingly impossible obstacles that might stand in the way of following His plan. As you continue to seek the Lord for wisdom and obey Him each step of the way, He will remove each obstacle in ways that will amaze you.

For example, I remember once when God began to deal with me two years ahead of time about pastoring a particular church. I began picking this church up in my spirit, and I asked the Lord, "Are You talking to me about pastoring that church?"

As I continued to pray about the matter, I became convinced that the Lord wanted me to pastor that particular church.

Then I prayed, "Lord, I see some major obstacles blocking the way of my ever pastoring that church. From the natural standpoint, those obstacles look like insurmountable mountains. So You'll have to work it out so I *can* pastor there."

Some of the leaders at that particular church were opposed to my ministry because of the message of faith and healing that I preached. They had tried to confront me in the past, wanting to fuss and argue with me about what *they* believed. But I just kept quiet and let *them* fuss. (I decided long ago that I'm going to walk in love whether anyone else does or not!)

So I told the Lord, "I'm not going to take what You've told me about pastoring that church and try to make it happen myself. I'm not going to say a word to anyone. I'm just going to stay committed to the church I'm pastoring now while I watch *You* work it out."

And God did just that! To my utter surprise, two

years later those leaders who had so adamantly opposed me were the very ones who asked me to come and pastor that church! God took care of every obstacle as I continued to pray and trust Him with the matter.

But the reason I could trust God to work out the situation is that I first sought Him in prayer until I had it clear in my spirit that pastoring *that* particular church was God's will for me.

Practical Insights To Praying Out The Mystery of God's Plan

It's so important to learn to wait before the Lord and pray out the mystery of God's plan for our lives. One way we can do that is to pray in other tongues.

The Bible says when we pray in tongues, we are praying *mysteries* to God: *"For he that speaketh in an unknown tongue speaketh not unto men, but unto God: for no man understandeth him; howbeit in the spirit he speaketh mysteries"* (1 Cor. 14:2). *Moffatt's* translations says we are praying *"divine secrets* in the Spirit."

Many of the bad things that happen to us — or the good things that should have happened but didn't — are a result of our failing in the past to pray out God's plan. You see, God has planned many things for us in the future that as we pray in the Spirit we will be praying out ahead of time. (We can pray in the Spirit both in tongues and in our native language when we pray by the unction of the Holy Spirit.)

In fact, what is happening in your life in the present, whether good or bad, is a result of what you have or have not prayed out in days gone by. And what will happen in your life in the future will be a result of your *present* prayer life.

At times, the Holy Spirit will impress you to pray about certain things that concern His plan for your life. You'll have an anointing or unction of the Holy Spirit to pray. But if you ignore the Holy Spirit's promptings and busy yourself with natural affairs, that anointing will leave, and you'll wonder if you ever sensed it! If you keep ignoring the Holy Spirit's promptings, you'll grieve the Holy Ghost, and He won't deal with you anymore about that issue.

So determine to always stay sensitive to those gentle promptings of the Holy Spirit. Take the time to wait upon the Lord in prayer and in the Word to discover His guidance and direction for your life. Wait long enough before Him until your mind becomes quiet and is no longer active. Wait long enough in prayer for all of your physical senses and emotions to be brought into captivity so they no longer dominate you. Then you'll be able to hear from your spirit.

Also, as you spend time in God's Presence, ministering to the Lord in praise and worship will quiet your mind and strengthen your spirit. That's why spending much time ministering to the Lord will greatly aid you in developing your spirit.

What does ministering to the Lord mean? It means to linger in His Presence, loving and worshipping Him for all that He is and for all He has done for you. It means to drink in of His glory and power and to let Him saturate every part of your being.

Ministering to the Lord will also help you hear from Him. For instance, in Acts 13:2, it says, *"AS THEY* [certain prophets and teachers at Antioch] *MINISTERED TO THE LORD, and fasted, THE HOLY GHOST SAID . . ."* (Acts 13:2). When you worship the Lord, you create the kind of atmosphere in which the Holy Spirit can speak to your heart.

As you spend time just loving and worshipping the Lord, it's so much easier to quiet your mind and emotions and focus on Jesus.

So if you want to experience intimate fellowship with the Lord and hear what He is saying to you, spend *much* time ministering to Him.

It can take some time to get your mind and body quiet. That's why the scripture says, *"BE STILL, and know that I am God . . ."* (Ps. 46:10).

Take the time to let your body become quiet. Let your mind be still. Let your emotions subside, until there's no emotion at all in manifestation coloring your thoughts. Once your mind and body are quiet, listen way down deep in your innermost being to what the

Holy Spirit is saying to you. Although at times your mind may seem to be in a fog, the Lord will enlighten your spirit and give you the guidance you need.

Don't allow yourself to become spiritually lazy and stop short of hearing what the Lord is saying to you in your spirit. If you become spiritually lethargic, you could end up following your own soulish desires, thinking all the time you're following God's plan for you.

You have to learn to distinguish between your soulish thoughts and desires and the Lord's leading in your spirit. To do that, you must become well-grounded in the Word, which is the only thing that can distinguish between soul and spirit (Heb. 4:12).

Becoming established in the Word will also help you learn to recognize the voice of Satan as well. The devil will try to speak subtle lies to your *mind* to deceive you (John 8:44; Rev. 12:9).

However, remember that God speaks to your *spirit*, and what He says to you will always line up with His Word. So always examine your leading in the light of the Bible. God will never lead you one step beyond the principles in His Word.

Also, examine your motives for taking the step you're considering. Ask yourself. *Why do I want to do this? Do I want to do it for my own selfish benefit or because someone else is doing it? Is this something my soulish nature wants to do or something God wants me to do?*

Sometimes it takes a considerable amount of time staying in the Presence of God for you to settle those questions. You can't always do it in one session of prayer.

Sometimes it takes long seasons of waiting before the Lord in prayer in order to get your motives pure and your priorities sorted out according to the Word so you can distinguish between the clamorings of your soul and the voice of your spirit.

But if you'll get still enough on the inside, and if you'll meditate on God's Word and pray in the Spirit long enough, you'll get deeper over into the Spirit, and you'll be able to differentiate between your soul and your spirit man. You'll be able to tell the difference between your *own* wants and desires and what *God* wants for you.

Then from way down inside of you, direction and guidance will rise up. And you'll be able to say with confidence, "Now I know what to do! This is the choice of the Lord. In times past, I was misled by my own emotions and my own human personality. But now I've heard from the Lord in my spirit. And although all the world might stand against me and say it's not so, I know what God wants me to do!"

And as you obey God's will and follow His plan, you'll enjoy the blessings He has provided for you.

The truth is, ministering to your own spirit — constantly feeding your spirit by meditating on the Word of

God and fellowshipping with the Lord — is the most important thing you can do to develop your spirit so you can ascertain God's will for your life. Only then can you live in the abundance God has provided for you.

Many Christians miss it by remaining in the mental and physical realms. Forgetting that the spiritual realm is the root, the stem, and the ground out of which all else grows, they get all agitated in their mind and emotions. And they run here and there, seeking for someone to give them mental, natural counsel.

But if they'd only stop, get quiet on the inside, and fellowship with the Lord, they'd begin to hear Him speak to their heart. Peace, contentment, and satisfaction would flow out of their spirit into their mind and emotions. All of their questionings would simmer down and become as nothing, and even their bodies would respond in joy and health.

Someone may say, "Well, I've been praying a long time, and I haven't heard anything yet." Then don't make a move until you do! Keep on seeking the Lord in the Word and in prayer.

Someone else may say, "I'm going to give God only this long to give me an answer. If He doesn't, I'll have to do it my way." No, it doesn't work that way. You can't give God *your* deadline! If you try, you'll be going the wrong direction for sure! You must wait before the Lord in faith that He will answer you in *His* time and in *His* way.

If you want to be led by the Holy Spirit, always be

willing to respond to His leading, even if it doesn't agree with your own human reasonings, expectations, or desires. Don't hinder your ability to discern His guidance through wrong thinking or selfish ambition. Stay teachable and open in your heart to anything the Lord may tell you. And as you do, He will teach you His ways and direct you into His plan for your life.

In my own life, I determined long ago to always respond instantly to the Holy Spirit's leading. And through the years, every time I took the time to seek the Lord for guidance in the Word and in prayer, God always gave me an answer. The Holy Spirit would bear witness with my spirit to God's plan, and I'd *know* on the inside I had received God's direction on the matter. I knew it better than I knew my own name!

You can experience the same success in receiving guidance from the Holy Spirit. But I want to emphasize this fact: Knowing the will of God and walking *in* the will of God is contingent upon your prayer life and upon being established in the Word.

The more time you spend waiting before the Lord in the Word and in prayer, the more sure you will be of the next step to take. In God's Presence, what is not of God in your life will gradually fall away.

You'll come to the place where you won't be bothered any more by those weights and sins that caused you to stumble in the past. And you'll find that you are able to walk in the clearly defined will of the Father.

As you practice praying out the mystery of God's plan for your life according to the Word, the Lord will take you deeper in the realm of prayer than you've ever been before.

I'm not talking about some mystical realm where you float around like a cloud in the sky and are too spiritual to be any earthly good! I'm talking about learning to enjoy a more intimate level of communion with the Lord. The things of the Spirit of God will become more real to you than the natural world around you.

That's the way it should be for every believer. Walking in the Spirit should be normal for the child of God. It should be as natural for a believer to be led by the Holy Spirit and to walk by faith as it is for fish to swim in the sea and birds to fly in the sky.

You see, you can become so attuned to the Holy Spirit who dwells inside you that in every situation of life, you'll know exactly what He is saying to you as you seek Him for guidance and direction. You'll develop a working relationship with God.

What do I mean by *a working relationship*? I mean you'll become so intimate with your Heavenly Father that it will become natural to talk everything over with Him just as a child would talk with his earthly father. You won't make any significant decisions without asking Him first, and He won't do anything that concerns you without telling you first.

Throughout my own Christian walk, I've developed

that kind of intimate, working relationship with the Lord. I've kept myself consecrated to God's will, whatever it may be. But I've always felt free to talk with Him just like a son would talk to his father.

For instance, on some matters that weren't that crucial, I've asked the Lord, "If it's all right with You, could I do it this way?" And the Lord told me, "That's fine with Me. It's not exactly what I had in mind, but if you want to do it that way, it's all right."

On the other hand, there have been times when the Lord told me, "No, don't ask to do that. It wouldn't be best." So I've trusted His wisdom and obeyed Him.

You can have an intimate relationship with the Lord if you'll stay in the Word, stay "prayed up," and stay yielded to the Holy Spirit's leading. God wants you to develop your spirit so you can enjoy close communion with Him. And as you wait in His Presence in prayer, in that holy place of sweet communion, at times you will catch glimpses in the Spirit of His plan for you as He shows you things to come (John 16:13).

Don't Let Satan Thwart God's Plan for You!

As you spend time in the Presence of the Lord, not only will you enter into a new dimension of communion with Him, but you will also gain a greater understanding of your authority and power in the Name of Jesus to stop Satan's strategies in your life. [3] This is extremely important, because Satan will do his best to thwart God's purpose for your life from being fulfilled.

Has the Lord spoken to you by His Word and by His Spirit concerning His plan for you? Perhaps you've waited and waited for what He has said to your heart to come to pass, yet nothing has happened. You need to seek the Lord and determine if your lack of results is due to Satan's strategies against you. If that is the case, you must speak to your mountain — whatever problem or circumstance Satan is using against you — and command it to be removed in the mighty Name of Jesus (Mark 11:23).

You see, there are often spiritual battles in prayer that we must wage as we stand our ground on the Word against the enemy who wants to keep God's plan from coming to pass in our lives. I'm not talking about a mental or physical battle. I'm talking about standing against spiritual forces of darkness in the Name of Jesus as we fight the good fight of faith by the Word of God (Eph. 6:12; 1 Tim. 6:12).

As we exercise our God-given authority in Jesus' Name, we enforce the victory over the devil that Jesus already bought for us on the Cross (Col. 2:15; Heb. 2:14). That is the kind of warfare Paul was talking about in First Timothy.

1 TIMOTHY 1:18
18 This charge I commit unto thee, son Timothy, according to the prophecies which went before on

thee, that thou by them mightest WAR A GOOD WARFARE.

In my ministry, there have been times when it seemed like every demon in hell was ganging up on me to keep me from following God's plan for my life. For instance, the first five months after I left my last church and went into the field ministry, it seemed like I had to stand against more demons than I had the previous fifteen years put together.

Everywhere I turned, I encountered oppression and opposition from the enemy. The devil tried to keep me out of the place of ministry that God had planned for me, but I overcame by steadfastly exercising my authority in Jesus Christ in prayer. You see, the Bible calls it a good fight of faith because sometimes we have to *steadfastly* and with *perseverance* take our stand against the enemy (Eph. 6:11-18).

You can do the same thing in your life. For instance, if a spirit of depression or oppression has been causing your spirit to be sluggish and your mind to be unclear, you need to command the enemy to stop his operations against you in the Name of Jesus.

Command Satan's power to be broken over *every* area of your life. Stand your ground against the enemy's strategies with the Word of God and the mighty Name of Jesus.

At the same time, hold fast to your confession of

faith that God's purposes will prevail in your life. Begin to say, "The Lord has spoken to me and therefore, in the Name of Jesus it *shall* come to pass!"

When you walk in that realm of authority in Jesus Christ, no man, no enemy, no demon, and no circumstance will be able to stand between you and the fulfillment of God's purposes for your life. And as you determine to develop your spirit and to always follow the leading of the Holy Spirit, to a greater and greater degree you will walk in victory and experience the fullness of God's plan for you.

I've shared different ways the Holy Spirit may lead you and some scriptural principles that when acted upon will help you successfully follow the Holy Spirit's guidance. But remember, spiritual things require practice, just as natural things do.

So don't get in a hurry and become discouraged if you don't grow up and develop spiritual maturity in these matters overnight. You didn't develop mentally and physically overnight, did you?

You didn't enter first grade one week and graduate from high school the next week! You didn't mature overnight. In the same way, your spiritual development will take some time too.

So just continue to be diligent to seek the Lord for guidance and direction in your life. Remember to exercise your God-given authority in Jesus Christ to stop Satan's attempts to thwart God's plan for your life.

Most importantly, spend much time in God's Presence, meditating on His Word, worshipping Him, and praying in the Spirit.

Don't get upset because you miss it a few times. Just keep on growing spiritually and developing your spirit. Refuse to walk after your own natural mind, and ask the Lord to make *His* thoughts *your* thoughts. As you are rooted and grounded in the Word and take time to listen to your spirit, the Bible promises that you *will* learn to be led by the Holy Spirit!

[1] For further study on the subject of how to be led by the Holy Spirit, see also How You Can Be Led by the Spirit of God by Rev. Kenneth E. Hagin.

[2] For further study on the subject of the baptism in the Holy Spirit with the evidence of speaking in tongues, see also The Holy Spirit and His Gifts by Rev. Kenneth E. Hagin.

[3] For further study on the subject of the authority of the believer, see also *The Believer's Authority* by Rev. Kenneth E. Hagin.

Chapter 5
Different Ways
The Holy Spirit Leads

*Howbeit when he, the Spirit of truth, is come,
he will guide you into all truth: for he shall not
speak of himself; but whatsoever he shall hear,
that shall he speak: and he will shew you things
to come.*

— John 16:13

We've talked about the three primary ways the Holy
Spirit leads believers: through the inward witness, the
still small voice, and the authoritative Voice of the Holy
Spirit. But now I want to give you some examples of
these various ways the Holy Spirit leads as we follow
His plan for our lives.

God Will Personally Lead You

First of all, however, let me stress that receiving
God's direction for your life is your own personal
responsibility. God wants to personally lead and guide
you in every area of your life so you can successfully
run the spiritual race He has set before you.

God isn't going to lead and guide you through other
people, although sometimes He will use someone else to

confirm what you already have in your own spirit. He's going to lead you by *His Spirit.*

Some Christians aren't willing to take the responsibility of seeking God's guidance for themselves. They are looking for an easy way out. They don't want to depend on their own personal relationship with God, because it takes time and effort to develop spiritually. They'd rather have someone else seek God for them and tell them what to do. Folks like that miss God's best for their lives, because God isn't going to lead them through other people. Besides, God desires to have a personal relationship with each one of His children.

God didn't call any of us to tell other people what to do. Although we might help someone by giving wise counsel according to the Word and the Holy Spirit, God wants His children to be led by the Holy Spirit who dwells inside each of them.

How different life would be for people if they would just accept the responsibility to hear and heed what the Holy Spirit is saying to each of them! So many trials and difficulties can be avoided if a person will just learn to follow the Holy Spirit's guidance.

In Acts chapter 27, we can see a biblical example of a great trial people encountered because they didn't heed the warning of the Holy Spirit. The Holy Spirit gave Paul, a prisoner on a ship bound for Rome, wise counsel about impending danger. Actually, Paul may have been the only one on board who was in a position to hear from God. He warned those in charge of the voyage that there was danger ahead.

ACTS 27:10-14,20,21

10 And [Paul] said unto them, Sirs, I PERCEIVE that this voyage will be with hurt and much damage, not only of the lading and ship, but also of our lives.

11 Nevertheless the centurion believed the master and the owner of the ship, more than those things which were spoken by Paul.

12 And because the haven was not commodious to winter in, the more part advised to depart thence also, if by any means they might attain to Phenice, and there to winter; which is an haven of Crete, and lieth toward the south west and north west.

13 And WHEN THE SOUTH WIND BLEW SOFTLY, supposing that they had obtained their purpose, loosing thence, they sailed close by Crete.

14 But not long after there arose against it a tempestuous wind, called Euroclydon....

20 And when neither sun nor stars in many days appeared, and no small tempest lay on us, all hope that we should be saved was then taken away.

21 But after long abstinence Paul stood forth in the midst of them, and said, Sirs, ye should have hearkened unto me, and not have loosed from Crete, and to have gained this harm and loss.

Notice that in verse 10 Paul did *not* say, "The Holy Ghost spoke to me." He said, "I *perceive*." Paul must have had an inward witness or spiritual perception that danger lay ahead of them if they ventured any further seaward before winter.

If the men in charge of the voyage would have listened to Paul, they could have saved their ship! But they wouldn't listen. Circumstances seemed favorable; the south wind was softly blowing, so they set sail.

But soon a huge storm came upon the ship and its passengers. The storm was the danger Paul had sensed in his spirit before they launched out. Because of the storm, all of the merchandise was lost. The ship was lost. Every man on board would have been lost, too, if those in charge hadn't decided to heed Paul's words before the ship ran aground (Acts 27:22-26,30-38).

Because those men finally did listen to what the Holy Spirit told Paul, God spared the life of every person on the ship (Acts 27:44). But how much better it would have been if they had listened to what God was saying through Paul to begin with!

The same thing still happens today. Often folks only start listening to God when they get in the middle of one of life's storms and they have nowhere else to turn. They get themselves in a situation where they are either going to listen to God and obey His direction, or they're going under.

The storms of life come to us all. However, some storms can be avoided altogether if we would just listen to the Lord's leading in the first place!

We have a choice. Yes, we can wait until the storm winds of life are tossing us all about and then start listening to the Holy Spirit. But how much better if we'd choose to heed His promptings while the south wind blows softly and everything is going smoothly so we can avoid the storm!

So take the responsibility to discern the Lord's leading for yourself. Learn to detect and follow the inward witness of the Holy Spirit. You have a Helper within you who will help you avoid unnecessary detours and pitfalls in life, and He will guide you safely along the path of God's plan as you seek the Lord with all of your heart.

The Inward Witness

Let me give you some examples of the ways the Holy Spirit leads His children. I'll also give you some practical principles to help you follow the leading of the Holy Spirit in your own life.

I could relate hundreds of instances in my own life and ministry that show how the Holy Spirit guided me by *the inward witness*, the primary way God leads His people.

For example, I knew by the inward witness that I was to start RHEMA Bible Training Center some time before I spoke it out by the unction of the Holy Spirit at Campmeeting '73. I was just as sure by the inward witness that God wanted me to start a ministerial training school as I would have been if Jesus had appeared to me in a vision and told me to start it.

For instance, in 1950 Jesus did appear to me. In that vision, He talked to me about my ministry and gave me a special healing anointing. But I had just as much assurance by the *inward witness* that I should start a Bible training center as I had by a *vision* of Jesus that I was supposed to have a healing ministry. I just knew on the inside by the inward witness that it was God's will for me to start a ministerial training center, although I didn't want to do it at first.

It was also by the inward witness that I was led to RHEMA's present location in Broken Arrow. You see, during the first two years of the training center, we operated out of Sheridan Assembly, a church in Tulsa. We had no building of our own to start RHEMA. The first year we graduated only fifty-eight students, but the attendance quickly grew, and by the second year, we had to find facilities that could accommodate more students.

So in 1976 we started looking for a permanent location for RHEMA Bible Training Center. We knew the facilities we chose needed to have the capacity to be enlarged as the number of students increased. We didn't want to turn away hundreds of students every year.

Then a businessman friend told me, "I might have found a suitable place for the school in Broken Arrow." So my wife and I drove to Broken Arrow to check it out.

The moment we turned the corner and I saw the office building and warehouse (now the Kenneth Hagin Ministries Administration Building and Rooker Memorial Auditorium, respectively), I sensed the Holy Spirit's signal or quickening in my spirit. I knew by the inward witness that we had found the right location.

My wife had the same inward witness. We didn't experience any spectacular revelation. But on the inside of us, we both just *knew* that the Lord was saying, "This is it!"

So we bought the property and moved the ministry and the training center to Broken Arrow. That wasn't an easy decision to make. It was a giant step of faith for us. The property was mostly undeveloped, and we knew it would take a lot of money to build the RHEMA campus. But despite what it looked like in the natural, we obeyed God. And things have worked out well for us. In the years since we first moved our offices to Broken Arrow, we've built the present RHEMA campus step by step, accomplishing what many said couldn't be done. But it all started by obeying the inward witness of the Holy Spirit.

Here's a side note to that account which will show you how important it is to heed the inward witness. Years ago I learned from an elderly Pentecostal woman how Pentecost had first come to Broken Arrow in the early 1900s. She told me about a young farm boy named Rupert Bailey who was baptized in the Holy Spirit in Broken Arrow's first Pentecostal church. This young man used to live on a farm located where RHEMA Bible Training Center stands today.

Although Rupert was just a teenager, he had a strong desire to see revival in his generation and in the generations to come. When Rupert wasn't working with his father on the farm, he would spend hours praying on a grassy knoll, located where Student Development Center 1 was later built. Day after day, he would pray and travail for lost souls.

One day after praying, Rupert stood up on that grassy knoll and prophesied by the unction of the Holy Spirit, "From this very spot, there will come a great work of God that will reach the world!"

Glory to God! No wonder when I saw that property, it was as if the Holy Spirit set off an electrical charge in my spirit! Obeying that inward witness to purchase the Broken Arrow property was instrumental in causing the word of the Lord, which was prophesied almost a century ago, to come to pass! And it was also an important step in successfully following God's plan for my life and ministry in these last days.

Success is always the result of following the leading of the Holy Spirit. Jesus once told me when He appeared to me in a vision, "If you will learn to follow the inward witness, I will make you rich [abundantly supplied]. I will guide you in all the affairs of life, financial as well as spiritual." The Lord is interested in every area of our lives. He wants us to prosper and enjoy success as we follow His plan for our lives.

I remember a fellow who visited RHEMA in the mid-1970s who benefited greatly financially by following the inward witness. He told me that soon after World War II, he invested $14,000 in a chemical company. That was a lot of money back then.

This man related, "Both my CPA and my stock broker advised me not to invest in this company. But I had such a good feeling in my spirit about it that I went ahead and made the investment anyway."

That "good feeling" in the man's spirit was not a physical feeling. It was a spiritual perception — the inward witness of the Holy Spirit — encouraging him to invest the money.

For the first ten years after the man invested his money in the chemical company, it didn't look like he had made a wise investment. He explained, "At one time I could have sold my stock and gotten about half of my money back. Several years later, if I had sold my stock, I still would have only broken even and gotten back my original investment. I thought, *Well, I sure missed God on that investment!*"

But the man continued to follow the inward witness that had led him to invest the money in the first place. He had no change of direction in his spirit, so he just left his stock alone and watched to see what would happen to his investment. Many years later, this chemical company finally began to show signs of success.

By the time this man talked to me, thirty years had passed since he had first invested his money. He told me, "I still own that same stock in the chemical company. And if I sold my stock today, it's worth about four million dollars!"

Four million dollars is not a bad return on a $14,000 investment! Yet the first ten years it didn't seem like it was a good investment. For quite a while, the man thought he had missed God.

But that man *didn't* miss God! Thirty years isn't long in the eyes of God. In this case, it just took thirty years for the man to reap the full benefits of obeying the Holy Spirit's leading to invest that money.

It pays to follow the inward witness, no matter how long it takes to reap the benefits of your obedience. If you learn to follow it, you'll always come out on top of the situation.

The Lord doesn't always settle up His accounts every Saturday night or by the first of next year. But I'll tell you this: if you'll stay with the Lord, sooner or later, God's Word — *including the leading of the Holy Spirit* — *will* prevail and you will come out on top!

Obey the Checks in Your Spirit!

Now someone might say, "I'm *trying* to follow the inward witness. And I've made plans, thinking the Lord was leading me in that direction. But I still have an uneasiness in my spirit about it. What should I do?"

If you don't know for certain on the inside that you have the Lord's direction and timing, don't make a move. It may just mean you are to pray out His plan more fully or that you don't have His timing quite right.

Just stay steady and continue to seek Him for guidance until you are sure. Wait until you have a release in your spirit that it's time to move out in God's plan.

And if you begin to move in a certain direction and you get a check in your spirit, then stop! That check or unrest in your spirit is a stop sign from the Lord, and although *you* may not understand it at the time, He has good reason for giving it to you.

You see, God knows the future. And He'll give you a check in your spirit if He sees you moving in a direction that will cause you harm or that will hinder you from fulfilling His plan for your life.

When the Lord gives you a check in your spirit, it's of utmost importance that you seek God until you know what it means. If you don't and you keep walking in the same direction you're going, you'll invariably suffer the

consequences of not heeding the Holy Spirit's warning.
For instance, I've seen pastors miss it by failing to heed that check in their spirit. Instead of taking the time to seek God and to get their mind, emotions, and body quiet so they could hear what their spirit was saying, they made a wrong move in the ministry. Sometimes they even changed churches out of the will of God.

It took some of those pastors years to get back on track with God's plan for them. Others never did get back on track. Some of them continued to flounder in life and ministry because their wrong move made them start doubting their own ability to hear God correctly.

Thank God we *can* hear from God! But we need to seek Him until we're sure we *have* heard from Him! And if we miss it, we need to keep trusting Him to teach us how to hear Him more accurately the next time.

I'll share with you one instance of a pastor who missed it in his ministry. When I was twenty-two years old and pastoring my first Full Gospel church, I visited a Full Gospel pastor in a nearby town. When I drove up in front of the parsonage, to my amazement I saw the pastor's car hooked up to a trailer, which was piled high with all his furniture and belongings.

I walked over to the pastor and asked, "What's going on?"

The pastor answered, "I've resigned my church."

The instant he said that, I knew in my spirit by the inward witness that he was missing it. But I was barely twenty-two. This man was old enough to be my father. I wasn't going to just blurt out, "You're missing it!" unless God specifically told me to tell him that.

I thought to myself, *Doesn't he know he's missing it?* I helped him pack the last few items into the trailer. When everything was loaded, the pastor shook hands with me and told me good-bye.

Then the pastor said something that let me know he didn't know for sure whether or not he was doing the right thing. He said, "I sure hope I'm not missing it." I never will forget the look on his face and the sound of his voice when he said that. Then he shook his head, got in the car with his wife, and drove off.

I just stood there in the driveway, almost weeping. I felt so bad inside as I watched them drive off, out of the will of God. That pastor ought to have known on the inside that he was missing it, not because he was a minister, but because he was a child of God. Every child of God can expect to be led by the Holy Spirit.

I went home and told my wife, "Brother So-and-so resigned from his church and took a pastorate in another town."

My wife said, "Doesn't he know he's missing it?" You see, my wife isn't a preacher, but she also picked it up in *her* spirit that the pastor had missed God.

I answered, "He sure is! But it wasn't my place to tell him unless the Lord told me to tell him."

You see, you need to have wisdom in this area. I could tell by the way the pastor talked he wouldn't have accepted it even if I had told him that I sensed he was missing it. I knew God was trying to tell him to stay where he was. But if that pastor wouldn't listen to God, he surely wouldn't have listened to me, a pastor only half his age.

Another minister came and took the pastorate of the church this pastor had left. A number of unfortunate things happened over the following months. The end result was that seven months later, the first pastor who had resigned returned to that same church.

That pastor was never so glad in his life to get back to his church! And he stayed there as the pastor for many more years. But while he was gone, the church had suffered. Because of the problems during those seven months, his congregation had dwindled to half its original size. If the pastor had obeyed God and had stayed put in the first place, he could have avoided that mess. And instead of suffering, the congregation probably would have prospered spiritually and also increased in size.

Pastors aren't the only ones who sometimes fail to heed the check in their spirit and as a result suffer the consequences. I'm sure there are mistakes every one of us have made that we could have avoided if we had been sensitive enough in our spirit to hear the Holy Spirit's warning!

So if you are moving in a certain direction in your life and you have an uneasiness in your spirit, don't go any further. Stop and seek God to find out exactly what He is saying to your spirit.

Don't Seek Spectacular Guidance

On the other hand, if you *know* on the inside of you by the inward witness what God wants you to do, don't wait around for God to give you more spectacular guidance. Obey the inward witness.

In other words, when God is bearing witness with your spirit by the Holy Spirit to go in a certain direction, be careful you don't ignore the inward witness because you want God to lead you in a more spectacular and obvious way, such as by a vision or an angelic visitation. It's especially easy to do that when God is leading you in a direction your flesh doesn't want to go.

Although at times God does lead His children through visions and other spectacular guidance, it is not our responsibility to tell the Lord how to lead us. We have no scriptural right to seek visions, voices, or angels to speak to us.

However, we do have a right to claim what the Bible promises us. And the Bible promises that the Holy Spirit will lead and guide us into all truth (John 16:13; Rom. 8:14).

So we need to find out from the Word how God leads and guides us by His Holy Spirit. Then we must seek Him for guidance, in any way He may want to give it.

I made the mistake of doubting the inward witness and seeking more spectacular guidance when God dealt with me about returning to pastor the Farmersville church.

As I said, neither Oretha nor I wanted to go back to

that church. We loved the congregation, but we didn't like anything else about the town.

After Oretha and I agreed that the Lord was leading us to return to Farmersville, we just committed the matter into the Lord's hands to work it out.

Less than two months later, one of the board members of that church called me and said, "Our pastor just resigned. Would you consider coming back to pastor our church?"

I didn't tell the board member what the Lord had been saying to me. I just said, "Well, I don't know. You have a congregational government at your church. The people have something to say about it because they would have to vote me in."

"That's the reason we're calling you," the board member answered. "The people have been coming to the board members, saying, 'See if Brother Hagin will come back as pastor.'"

So I went back for a few days to preach in the Farmersville church. And while I was there, the congregation voted me back in as pastor.

But even though I knew on the inside that I was to be the next pastor, I let my mind start drifting back into the natural realm. I started thinking, *Do I really want to come back here? Except for the people, I can't think of one thing I like about this place.* And I began to doubt the inward witness.

So I tried to get God to give me more spectacular guidance by fasting for three days and by praying over

and over, "Oh, God, move! Speak to me!" I guess I
wanted Him to write me a message in the sky or paint
me a picture in the clouds! *At the very least,* I thought,
*a vision or a prophecy would help me to be sure of God's
will in this decision.*

I was in my third day of fasting and praying when
the Lord spoke to me. I was on my knees, praying, "Oh,
Lord, give me a sign!" when suddenly He spoke to me
by the still small voice.

The Lord said, "Get up from there! I'm not going to
give you any sign. You've just wasted your time, fasting
and praying for some kind of spectacular sign. You
already know on the inside of you what to do, so do it!"

I answered, "Yes, Lord!" And I never said another
word to Him about it. I just obeyed what He had
already told me and took the pastorate of the Farmersville church. And as it turned out, we were greatly
blessed for our obedience.

I learned a lesson from that experience. I never
sought spectacular guidance from the Lord again. It was
a long time after that experience before I ever had a
vision. But when I did, I wasn't praying for God to give
me one. I'd learned to be content with following the Holy
Spirit's guidance in any way He desired to lead me. And
most of the time, He leads me by the inward witness.

The Still Small Voice

I said that when I was fasting and praying about the
Farmersville church, the Lord spoke to me by the still

small voice. *The still small voice of our own spirit* is the second most common way the Lord leads His people by the Holy Spirit. My spirit was picking up the voice of the Holy Spirit, and that's how the Lord led me in that instance.

Let me give you another example in my own life when the Lord led me by the still small voice. In 1970 my wife and I were in New York holding meetings in various cities. One Sunday as I was taking our belongings into the hotel where we were staying, I began to feel physically sick.

Now if that happened to someone else, that might not mean a thing in the world. But, you see, thirty-six years earlier, I had been raised off the deathbed, and I hadn't had the flu or a headache in thirty-six years. (Now more than fifty-five years have passed, and I *still* haven't had the flu or a headache — and I don't ever intend to! I'm not bragging on myself. I'm bragging on Jesus! He's the Healer!)

In the past if symptoms of sickness tried to attack me, I would simply act on Mark 11:24, as I did when I first got healed. And always before when I prayed the prayer of faith, I would either be instantly healed, or I would immediately begin to feel better.

So I prayed the prayer of faith as I always had. But this time, I got no better fast!

When I got to the hotel room, I lay down on the bed, feeling like I would fall on the floor if I didn't. As I lay there, I began to seek the Lord to find out why my prayer of faith hadn't worked.

I said, "Lord, I didn't make my connection with You when I prayed. I know You don't miss it. You never change, and You never fail. So I know I've missed it somewhere. So tell me, Lord, where did I miss it?"

The Lord answered me, not by an audible Voice, but through the still small voice of my spirit. (My spirit picked up the voice of the Holy Spirit.) The Lord said, "Lay your own hands on yourself to be healed. Twenty years and four days ago, I appeared to you and told you, 'The healing power is in your *hands.*'"

So I didn't waste any time laying hands on myself! Immediately I felt a warm glow go out of my hands into my stomach and spread throughout my body. Instantly I began to feel better.

Then the Lord said to me, "You haven't done what you should have done with the healing ministry. That is part of your calling." You see, for about five years I had backed off of laying hands on the sick. But the healing ministry was part of God's plan for my life.

"Now go back to Tulsa and start over again," the Lord told me. "Tell the people what I said to you in the vision in 1950 — that I gave you a healing anointing to minister to the sick. And as you obey Me and begin to lay hands on the sick, a stronger healing anointing will come upon you to abide."

From that time on, I began obeying the Lord in regard to the healing ministry, and His words came to pass. I began to operate in a stronger healing anointing.

The Authoritative Voice of the Holy Spirit

Another way the Holy Spirit leads His people is by *the authoritative Voice of the Holy Spirit.* In my own life, there have been times when the Holy Spirit has spoken to my spirit in a Voice that seems to be audible, although other folks around me don't hear it.

Many times I've heard that authoritative Voice of the Holy Spirit, and I've asked people near me, "Did you hear that?" To me the Voice was that real. Usually, they say, "No, we didn't hear anything."

I'm of the opinion that Philip heard the audible Voice of the Holy Spirit in Acts 8:29: *"Then THE SPIRIT SAID unto Philip, Go near, and join thyself to this chariot."* Whether the Voice was audible to anyone else or not, I'm convinced that it was audible to Philip.

Another biblical example of the Holy Ghost's speaking to someone is found in Acts chapter 10.

Peter had just had a vision while praying on the housetop. In that vision, God told him that salvation through Jesus Christ was available to the Gentiles (Acts 10:10-16).

ACTS 10:19,20
19 While Peter thought on the vision, THE SPIRIT SAID UNTO HIM, Behold, three men seek thee.
20 Arise therefore, and get thee down, and go with them, doubting nothing: for I have sent them.

In all probability the Holy Spirit spoke to Peter by the authoritative Voice (v. 19). If you had been on that housetop with Peter, you probably would not have heard the Holy Spirit speak. But the authoritative Voice of the Holy Spirit was audible to Peter. He distinctly heard what the Holy Spirit said to him.

In my own experience, I have found this to be true: Most of the time when God audibly speaks to me by His Holy Spirit, it means rough sailing is ahead of me. The Lord tells me by the authoritative Voice of the Holy Spirit so I'll hold steady when the storm hits. When I don't need that kind of strong guidance to keep me steady, He doesn't usually speak to me that way. For the most part, when I don't need strong guidance, He just leads me by the inward witness.

For example, we see that principle in the passage we just read. Look what happened to Peter after the Holy Spirit spoke to him. As Peter preached the gospel to Cornelius and his entire household, God gloriously saved every one of them and baptized them in the Holy Ghost (Acts 10:44-46). But then Peter encountered some rough times spiritually.

After that supernatural experience with the Gentiles, Peter's actions were called into question by the other Jewish brethren. The Bible says that ". . . *when Peter was come up to Jerusalem, they that were of the circumcision contended with him*" (Acts 11:2). Peter had to defend what he had done in preaching the gospel to the Gentiles by explaining, ". . . *THE SPIRIT BADE ME GO . . .*" (Acts 11:12).

Apparently Peter needed the more spectacular guidance of the Holy Spirit through the authoritative Voice to hold him steady when he encountered opposition by the Jewish believers. At that time, the Jewish believers were opposed to the Gentiles being included in the New Covenant; they didn't know that was part of God's plan of redemption.

Several times in my own life and ministry when rough sailing was ahead, God has spoken to me in the authoritative Voice. For instance, in 1946 I was considering the possibility of taking the pastorate of a little church in Van, Texas.

One day I asked God what His will was in the matter. Immediately I heard the audible Voice of the Holy Spirit speak to my spirit. It was just as plain to me as if someone were standing beside me speaking.

The Voice said, "You are the next pastor at the Van church. And that will be the last church you will ever pastor."

I soon found out why the Lord spoke to me audibly. If He hadn't given me such obvious guidance, I would have left that church before I ever started pastoring it!

The church at Van was what preachers called "a troubled church." Because of various problems, the congregation of that church was divided into two groups.

I came with my family to preach so the congregation could vote on whether or not they wanted me as their pastor.

I quickly found out that it's not easy preaching to a congregation that has drawn an imaginary line down the middle of the church — one half on one side divided against the other half on the other side! The atmosphere was so cold and dead it seemed as if every word I preached bounced off the back wall like a rubber ball and hit me in the face.

I thought I was only going to preach Wednesday evening. But unknown to me, the board members had scheduled me to preach Wednesday through Sunday evening. That meant every night I had to move my family from one deacon's house to another deacon's house. Otherwise, the deacons would get jealous of each other! It would have been funny if it wasn't so pathetic.

I told my wife, "If I didn't know God was in this, I'd just pile us all into the car and leave town without telling anyone!" The only reason I stayed was that I wanted to obey God. But that's why God had spoken to me by the authoritative Voice of the Holy Spirit. It was to hold me steady in rough times.

The church members held their election that Sunday evening. I got every vote but two. Someone said, "Why, that's a miracle! These people don't agree on anything!"

But Jesus had told me I would be the next pastor of that church, so I wasn't surprised. I never told the congregation I'd heard a Voice from Heaven. I just got up and accepted the pastorate as graciously as I could, despite the fact that my mind and my physical senses were hollering to leave before I even got started!

The first six months of pastoring that church were tough. The former pastor was still in town. He would visit the half of the congregation who still favored him as pastor and collect their tithes for himself. And he'd tell any church member he met, "God can't bless that church because I'm supposed to be the pastor."

Once in a while this former pastor would hold a meeting in another town, and I'd have a little respite. I could always tell when he was gone. There would be a difference in the church services; the spiritual atmosphere lightened, and it was easier to preach.

No one had to tell me when the former pastor came back to town, either. I'd start preaching Sunday morning, and I'd immediately think, *Brother So-and-so is back in town.* The atmosphere was cold again, and I'd sense my words bouncing off the back wall like rubber balls.

I'd tell my wife after every Sunday night service, "If I didn't know God wanted me to pastor this church, I'd rent a truck, load all our belongings in it at midnight, and leave without even telling anyone we were going. They'd come by the next day, find the parsonage empty, and think the rapture had taken place!"

We struggled through those six months. It was tough, but things became easier as I stayed steady and walked in love toward the people, including that former pastor.

I determined I would endeavor to help this former pastor any way I could. And in the process of time, I had the opportunity to be a blessing to him.

Love always wins! This pastor and his wife were reconciled to the congregation and then went on to successfully establish a church in another town. And although the first several months at the Van church had been rough sailing for me and my family, over the next few years we were greatly blessed for obeying God.

Another time I heard the audible Voice of the Holy Spirit was in May 1950. I heard an audible Voice speak to me from Heaven in the English language. It was Jesus speaking through the Holy Spirit (John 16:13). Jesus said to me, "Thou shalt not die, but thou shalt live. I want you to go teach My people faith. I have taught you faith through My Word, and I have permitted you to go through certain experiences. You have learned faith both through My Word and by experience. Now go teach My people what I have taught you. Go teach My people faith!"

I have endeavored to be obedient to that heavenly Voice. That's one reason I teach so much about faith. I'm supposed to! For me, it's a part of my obedience to the will of God for my life.

After that supernatural experience, I obeyed God and went back into the field ministry. And in those early years of field ministry, I ran up and down the hills and hollows of east Texas, preaching about faith when no one else was. I was criticized, persecuted, and talked about, but it never fazed me in the least bit.

The Lord had given me a commission through the audible Voice of the Holy Spirit, so I just kept right on preaching about faith. I was determined to obey the Lord and follow His plan for my life, no matter what.

Those are just some examples of the many times in my life when the Lord has spoken to me in the authoritative Voice of the Holy Spirit in order to prepare me for what was coming in His future plans for me. That's scriptural.

God Will Show Us Things To Come

You see, God promises us in His Word that the Holy Spirit will show believers things to come: *"Howbeit when he, the Spirit of truth, is come, he will guide you into all truth . . . and HE WILL SHEW [show] YOU THINGS TO COME"* (John 16:13).

Believers can claim John 16:13 and expect God to reveal His plan for their individual lives.

Of course, the Lord won't show you *everything* that is to come. He isn't going to show you His entire plan for your life all at one time from the beginning to end. He wants you to walk by faith, not by sight (2 Cor. 5:7).

If He showed you everything, you'd be walking by *sight*, not by *faith*. And without faith you wouldn't be able to please Him (Heb. 11:6).

There will always be a certain amount of mystery to anything that is supernatural, including God's plan for our lives.

Even the Apostle Paul said, *"For we know in part, and we prophesy in part"* (1 Cor. 13:9). Paul also said, *". . . For now we see through a glass, darkly . . ."* (1 Cor. 13:12). That's where faith comes in as we walk with God.

But occasionally the Lord will give you a glimpse into the future. As you stay attuned to His Spirit, God will alert your spirit to those things to come that are necessary for you to know, so you can prepare yourself and be ready for His future plans for you.

Glimpses Into the Future
Through the Word of Wisdom

God can also reveal His plan for the future through the word of wisdom. The word of wisdom is one of the nine gifts of the Holy Spirit, listed in First Corinthians 12:8-10.

We can define the word of wisdom as *a supernatural revelation by the Spirit of God concerning the divine plan and purpose in the mind and will of God.* The word of wisdom can come through various means, such as dreams, visions, and the audible Voice of the Holy Spirit.

A distinct characteristic of the word of wisdom is that it always speaks of the future. It could be given to reveal part of God's future plans, to give guidance to a believer, or to confirm a divine call.

Although the word of wisdom usually occurs in more spectacular and frequent demonstration in the office of the prophet, it can sometimes occur in other believers' lives as the Spirit wills. However, regardless whether or not a layperson ever receives a word of wisdom, *all* believers *can* expect the Holy Spirit to give them guidance about things to come in their lives according to John 16:13.

Let me give you a biblical example of an instance when God gave someone a word of wisdom. God gave Joseph a word of wisdom to reveal His future plans for him. When Joseph was still a teenager, God gave him a glimpse into the future through two dreams. Joseph dreamed that someday he would rule over his brothers and even his parents (Gen. 37:5-10).

Joseph's brothers were jealous of him and sold him as a slave to the Ishmaelites (Gen. 37:27,28). Although the Lord prospered Joseph even in slavery, eventually Joseph was falsely accused and cast into prison (Gen. 39:7-20).

Joseph spent many years in prison. Ordinarily, a man would become bitter after spending all that time in prison for an unjust cause. Most people would have given up and forgotten what God had told them.

You see, when the Lord gives someone a word of wisdom, often the person has no idea how long it will take for that word to come to pass. Also, he doesn't necessarily know what else must take place in order for it to be fulfilled. Or it could come to pass in an entirely different way than the person expected it to.

That's why it's important for the believer to leave the fulfillment of a word of wisdom in the Lord's hands and just stay in faith about what the Lord has told him.

That's what Joseph did. For years everything looked hopeless, but Joseph remained true to God. And because Joseph stayed faithful to God, the word of wisdom he had received as a teenager finally came to pass.

God highly promoted Joseph, making him prime minister of the greatest nation of that day (Gen. 41:38-41). And eventually Joseph witnessed the fulfillment of the dreams he'd received from the Lord when his brothers bowed down to him as Egypt's second in command (Gen. 42:6).

I could share several examples from my own life of instances when the Lord has given me guidance through a word of wisdom. Sometimes the word of wisdom has come through the authoritative Voice of the Holy Spirit.

Several times God has awakened me at dawn by the audible Voice of the Holy Spirit and told me something about the future so I could prepare for what was to come.

For example, in 1956 I was holding meetings in California. As the sun came up one morning, I suddenly sat up in bed; it was just as if someone had touched me. I heard the audible Voice of the Holy Spirit speaking as clearly as if a person were standing in my bedroom. I heard these words: "A recession is coming — not a depression — but a recession. Get ready for it."

In the months following that experience, I didn't prepare as I should have. And because I didn't heed the Holy Spirit's warning, I ended up suffering financially. However, God later helped me recover from the financial fix I had gotten myself into because I hadn't listened to Him.

A similar incident occurred in 1974, but this time I obeyed what the Holy Spirit told me to do. It was the first year of RHEMA Bible Training Center when we were still at Sheridan Assembly in Tulsa.

One morning at 5:45, I sat straight up in bed. The Lord said to me, "An economic crunch is coming to the nation. Get ready for it. If you'll do what I tell you to do, you'll feel the effects of the crunch, but it won't affect you as it does other people."

I wrote down exactly what the Lord instructed me to do. The Lord said, "Number one, stop operating in outreaches I never told you to get involved with in the first place. Number two, trim your payroll by laying off this many people from your staff (and He told me exactly how many people to lay off). Number three, cut back on expenses. Operate the ministry on ninety percent of your incoming cash flow and save the other ten percent."

I immediately set about obeying the Lord's instructions. I called my son-in-law, Buddy, who was my office manager at the time, and told him, "I want to meet with every employee at 2:00 this afternoon."

When I went to the meeting, I took the piece of paper on which I had written down the words the Lord had spoken to me. I told the employees, "Now, folks, I'm going to have to tell you what the Lord said to me this morning." And I read what I had written.

I said to them, "I'm going to do exactly what the Lord told me to do. I've never gotten in trouble listening to Him. In fact, every time I *haven't* listened to Him, I've always gotten into trouble. I don't want to suffer the consequences of disobeying Him."

So I followed the Lord's instructions. We laid off the number of employees the Lord told us to. We also got out of the various outreaches the Lord never told me to begin. Because I obeyed the Lord, everything worked out well.

I also began saving ten percent of the ministry income as God had directed me. Then in 1976, we real-

ized we would have to purchase property for the new
RHEMA campus and ministry headquarters. If I hadn't
obeyed God and started saving that ten percent back in
1974, we wouldn't have had the money on hand to buy
the property in Broken Arrow!

God warned us of things to come by a word of wisdom
through the authoritative Voice of the Holy Spirit, and we
obeyed His instructions. Because of the Lord's instruction
to us, this ministry only felt a little of the economic pressure that came upon the entire nation in 1975.

We came through the economic crunch without suffering financially, and we were able to fulfill God's plan
to move to our new location in Broken Arrow. Obedience to God always brings benefits!

In guiding believers into God's plan for their lives,
the Holy Spirit may also give a person a word of wisdom to assure him of his divine call and commission.

For instance, I once heard about the Lord supernaturally giving a word of wisdom through tongues and
interpretation to a missionary woman to confirm her
call. This woman had ministered in India for seven
years before returning in a discouraged state of mind to
the United States.

One day this missionary woman was speaking about
missions at a small Bible college. Suddenly one of the
students stood up and began to speak in other tongues.
Everyone waited, but no interpretation came forth.
However, the missionary woman, who was sitting on
the platform, began to weep. She was obviously deeply
affected by the message in tongues.

Finally, the missionary stood up and came to the pulpit. "We don't need an interpretation for that message. That message in tongues was for me!" the woman exclaimed. "That person was speaking in the dialect of the Indian people to whom I ministered for seven years.

"You see, my mission board doesn't know it yet, but I've been traveling and speaking around the country to raise money for *other* missionaries. It was my intention never to return to India.

"But God just spoke to me and confirmed my call through that message in tongues. The Lord said, 'I called you to India. You are to go back and minister there.'" Then the missionary woman related to the students what the Lord had told her in that message in tongues about her future ministry in India.

Through a word of wisdom, God gave that missionary woman supernatural guidance and confirmed her call to India. The woman did return to India. In fact, she spent thirty-five more years there, obeying the will of God for her life.

I've given you several examples from the Word, my own life, and the lives of others to show you some of the ways the Holy Spirit leads us in order to unfold His plan for our lives.

Remember, the primary way the Lord leads us is by the inward witness. He might also choose to lead us in more spectacular ways, but we are not to seek voices, dreams, or visions. We only need to seek the Lord, expecting to be led by the Holy Spirit as the Bible promises.

You have a personal responsibility to wait before the

Lord in the Word and in prayer in order to receive His direction for your life. Just trust the Holy Spirit to give you guidance in whatever way *He* sees fit.

Stay sensitive to His leading and obey what He tells you to do to prepare for what is to come. If you'll keep yourself willing and obedient, He'll take you step by step into the fullness of God's plans and purposes for your life!

Chapter 6
Obeying God Doesn't Cost — It Pays!

Years ago when I was in the field ministry, I drove to most of my meetings. At the time it was more convenient to drive so I could take all my teaching books and tapes with me on the road.

Once my wife and I were traveling through Missouri, and we saw a large billboard on the turnpike that read: "It doesn't cost; it pays." The message on that billboard was referring to advertising, but I said to my wife, "You could apply that spiritually too. It doesn't cost to surrender to God; it *pays*."

Some Christians, bless their darling hearts, are always talking about what *they* had to give up and what it cost *them* to be a Christian. I'd just as soon hear a donkey bray at midnight in a tin barn than to hear folks talk like that!

It doesn't *cost* to obey God and to dedicate your life to Him. It *pays*! It will cost you *not* to obey God. It may cost you in dollars and cents. It may cost you sickness, disease, and premature death. It may cost you heartache and sorrow. But, oh, thank God, it's so good over in the perfect will of God, where you're fully surrendered, fully dedicated, fully submitted to the will of God! It's just so much better to obey God than to disobey Him.

Disobedience Puts the Light Out

A person can disobey something specific that God told him to do. That's disobedience. But a person can disobey the *Bible*, God's revealed will, and that's disobedience too. And it will cost him.

For example, I remember when God first began to deal with me about the sin of worry. I was on my deathbed, paralyzed because of a deformed heart and an incurable blood disease. I had to deal with the sin of worry before I could receive healing for my body in faith, because worry and anxiety hinder a person's faith.

I was just a fifteen-year-old boy. You may say that a child couldn't worry. But, yes, children *can* worry. Children are just replicas, so to speak, of their parents and what they see their parents do.

I learned to worry at a very early age. My mother and grandmother were *world-champion* worriers, and I probably came in third place right behind the two of them!

I was born again on my deathbed, and I had promised God that I would never doubt anything I read in His Word. But as I began to read the Scriptures, I got bogged down in Matthew chapter 6, and it took me six months to get out of that chapter because I was under such conviction about it.

MATTHEW 6:25,27,28,31
25 Therefore I say unto you, TAKE NO THOUGHT
for your life, what ye shall eat, or what ye shall
drink; nor yet for your body, what ye shall put on.
Is not the life more than meat, and the body than
raiment. . . .

27 Which of you by TAKING THOUGHT can add one cubit unto his stature? 28 And why TAKE YE THOUGHT for raiment? Consider the lilies of the field, how they grow; they toil not, neither do they spin.... 31 Therefore TAKE NO THOUGHT, saying, What shall we eat? or, What shall we drink? or, Wherewithal shall we be clothed?

I had promised the Lord I would never doubt anything I read in His Word. I told Him, "When I read Your Word and understand it, I promise You that I will put it into practice." But when I got to Matthew 6, spiritually speaking, the light seemed to grow dim because I didn't put Matthew 6 into practice.

You may say, "Well, I never made any promise to God never to doubt His Word and to always put into practice what I read and understand."

But if you are saved, you're not supposed to doubt God's Word. Some people think if they don't commit themselves to be faithful to God's Word, then they're safe in disobeying it. But if you're a child of God, God still requires faith of you whether you've committed yourself to believe Him or not.

Matthew 6:25 says, ". . . *Take no thought for your life.* . . ." The Bible I was reading while on my deathbed had a little footnote at the bottom that read, "Do not be anxious about tomorrow." In other words, Jesus Himself was saying, "Do not worry!"

When I realized what the Lord was dealing with me about, I said in astonishment, "Why, Lord, if I have to live like that, I'll never make it as a Christian." I thought I couldn't live without worry or without being anxious, so I shut my Bible.

Up until then, everything in God's Word had been all clear and light and a blessing to me. But when I chose not to walk in the light of what God showed me in His Word, everything became dark and fuzzy and unclear to me.

I thought to myself, *I'll keep reading, but I'll just skip Matthew 6.* So I kept on reading. I even began to study about the antichrist! The subject of the antichrist was not a problem area with me, so it didn't convict me when I read about it. But worrying *was* a problem, and my conscience smote when I read about it, because I wasn't practicing the Word in that area.

You see, you're not going to get any more light from God until you walk in the light you already have. So don't be concerned about the things you don't understand in God's Word; just see to it that you practice what you do know. The rest of it will take care of itself.

Finally, I said to the Lord, "Forgive me for worrying and for being full of anxiety. I know You will forgive me because First John 1:9 says if I confess my sin to You, You are faithful and just to forgive me and to cleanse me from all unrighteousness. I promise You, Lord, that I'll never worry again the longest day I live."

God as my witness, many years have come and gone, and although I've been sorely tempted, I have not worried.

It just pays to obey God and His Word. In fact, if you are not walking in the light of God's *Word*, it will be very difficult for you to walk in God's specific will for you and to follow His plan and purpose for your life.

Dear friend, God has a perfect plan for your life, and that plan includes walking in the light of His specific will for you. But it also includes walking in the light of His holy written Word.

Healing Is Part of God's Plan for Your Life

For example, it is God's perfect plan for you to walk in divine health. Now if you do get sick, there is healing for you, but God's best is that we walk in health.

God doesn't have any less for us under the New Testament than He did for His people under the Old Testament. In fact, the Bible says that in Christ we have a new and better covenant established upon better promises (Heb. 8:6).

In the Old Testament, God said to Israel, "I'll take sickness away from the midst of you" (Exod. 23:25).

> **EXODUS 23:25,26**
> **25 And ye shall serve the Lord your God, and he shall bless thy bread, and thy water; and I WILL TAKE SICKNESS AWAY FROM THE MIDST OF THEE.**
> **26 There shall nothing cast their young, nor be barren, in thy land: THE NUMBER OF THY DAYS I WILL FULFIL.**

Notice the Lord didn't tell the Israelites they would never die. He said, "The number of your days I will *fulfill*." That meant that they would live and die without sickness and disease, because in the previous verse, He said, "I'll take sickness away from the midst of you."

Some people in their natural thinking ask, "Well, if that's true — if the Israelites could live free from sickness and disease — then how would they ever die?"

The Old-Testament patriarchs who walked under the provision of the covenant didn't die sick or diseased. They just sort of wore out, bless God! Many times they would call in their children first and lay hands on them and bless them. Then they would just say, "It's time for me to go," and they gave up the ghost and went on to glory!

"Yes," someone said, "but that's under the Old Testament. That only belonged to Israel. It doesn't belong to the Church." But we just read that in Hebrews 8:6 it says that in Christ we have a new and better covenant established upon *better promises!* How much better is the New Covenant than the old Covenant if they had the privilege of living free from sickness and disease, but we don't have that same privilege?

I saw a sign in a pastor's office in a church where I held a meeting, and it read: "I was rich, and I was poor. *Rich* is better." I paraphrased that to say: "I was well, and I was sick. *Well* is better."

Since we have a new and better covenant established on better promises, it has to include all that the Old Covenant had and more, or else it wouldn't be better.

Obedience Has Its Price

Notice that God's promise of healing to the Israelites was conditional. It was conditional upon their dedicating and submitting themselves to God's Word and to God Himself. When they dedicated and submitted themselves to God and His Word, He kept His part of the covenant and took sickness away from their midst and caused them to enjoy long life on the earth.

You see, it doesn't cost to obey God and His Word; it *pays*.

God wants us to submit to His Word, which is His revealed will to man. But He also wants us to submit to His will or plan for our individual lives. I'm talking about fulfilling your place of service in the Kingdom of God. If you will obey God in every area of your life, it won't cost you; it will pay off!

I once heard a minister say, "Preaching or teaching the Bible or discussing Bible truths is like climbing a mountain. If you climb up one side of the mountain, you have one view. If you climb up the other side, you have another view entirely."

That is certainly true. For instance, preachers will often minister on the love of God, and that's scriptural. Thank God, God *is* love. The Bible says God is love (1 John 4:8). But did you know the same Bible also says God is a flaming fire (Deut. 4:24; Heb. 12:29)? Did you know that the Bible also says judgment begins at the house of God and that if the righteous are barely saved, what will become of the godless and the wicked? (1 Peter 4:17,18)?

Many people don't like to hear about the judgment side of God. They would rather hear that God is love and that they can do anything they want to do — cuss, smoke, drink, commit adultery — and God will just sort of wink at it. People who do things like that are not dedicated to God in the least. They are dedicated to the flesh, the world, and the devil.

Certainly, God is love. The Bible says, *"For God so loved the world, that he gave his only begotten Son, that whosoever believeth in him should not perish, but have everlasting life"* (John 3:16). God gave us the gift of His Son, but what have we done with the gift? To reject God and His Word brings judgment. Folks bring judgment on themselves when they persist in disobeying God and His Word.

Some people think they can do anything they want to do and live any way they want to and God will still love them. Thank God, He does, but there's still a penalty for wrongdoing.

If you fall away from God and then repent and turn to Him, God loves you enough to take you back and cleanse you and straighten you up if you'll let Him. But if you persist in wrongdoing and disobedience, it's going to cost you.

Many times, bad things happen to folks, and they ask, "Did God do this?" No, oftentimes people open the door to the devil through their own disobedience.

Don't misunderstand me. Just because you're experiencing tests and trials doesn't necessarily mean you're in disobedience. The devil will try to attack you even when you're in the center of God's perfect will. He will try to see what you're made of spiritually and if you really believe what you say you believe about the Word.

But if you'll stand your ground in faith on God's Word, payday will come, because it doesn't cost to obey God and be faithful to Him and His Word; it *pays!*

It pays to serve God! It pays to surrender to the Lord! It pays to dedicate your life — all that you are, all that you have, all you ever expect to be — to God.

God Rewards Faithfulness

In surrendering to the Lord and letting Him have His way in our lives, sometimes it seems costly right at the moment, because there is often a price to pay on our part to obey God. But, thank God, in the long run, it pays well and good to obey God.

Let me give you an illustration from the Bible to show you that even though God's plan may not seem easiest at the moment, in the end it always pays to obey God. In Genesis chapters 37 through 50 we read the account of Joseph and the price he had to pay to obey God.

You know the problems Joseph had. God had given Joseph dreams about His plan for his life. Joseph's brothers got jealous of him and wanted to kill him, but one brother intervened, and they sold Joseph into slavery instead. Then they told their father, Jacob, that a wild beast had devoured their brother.

Joseph went to Egypt as a slave, and after much persecution and hardship spent seven years in jail for a crime he didn't commit. Then he interpreted dreams for Pharaoh's chief butler and baker. He told the butler that his dream meant he would be restored to his position, and he told the baker that his dream meant he was going to be beheaded.

Joseph asked the butler to remember him when he was restored to favor, but the butler forgot about Joseph. Joseph had already spent five years in prison at that time. And he spent another two years locked up before he was finally released.

When Joseph realized the butler had forgotten about him, Joseph had the opportunity to give up on the dream God had given him. But instead he remained faithful. If that would have been most folks, Joseph would have said something like, "I obeyed God, and I did a favor for the butler, and what do I get? *Forgotten.* It just doesn't pay to serve God."

But Joseph remained faithful, and later when Joseph interpreted Pharaoh's dream, he got promoted to prime minister of Egypt!

Joseph's obedience paid off, although I'm sure at times the price seemed too great to pay to walk in God's will for his life.

When a drought came and there was a famine throughout Israel, Joseph's father, Jacob, sent his sons to Egypt to buy grain. He didn't send his youngest son, Benjamin, however. Joseph and Benjamin were his youngest sons, born to him by Rachel. Jacob had already lost Joseph, and he didn't want to lose Benjamin too.

Joseph recognized his brothers when they came to buy grain, but they didn't recognize him. At first, Joseph accused his brothers of being spies and spoke harshly to them. Joseph was working a plan to try to see his father and his brother, Benjamin, again.

GENESIS 42:12-15,19,20,24
12 And he [Joseph] said unto them, Nay, but to see the nakedness of the land ye are come.
13 And they said, Thy servants are twelve brethren, the sons of one man in the land of Canaan; and, behold, the youngest is this day with our father, and one is not.
14 And Joseph said unto them, That is it that I spake unto you, saying, Ye are spies:
15 Hereby ye shall be proved: By the life of Pharaoh ye shall not go forth hence, except your youngest brother come hither. . . .
19 If ye be true men, let one of your brethren be bound in the house of your prison: go ye, carry corn for the famine of your houses:
20 But bring your youngest brother unto me; so shall your words be verified, and ye shall not die. . . .
24 . . . and [Joseph] took from them Simeon, and bound him before their eyes.

The brothers returned home to their father, Jacob, with a limited supply of grain and told him everything that had happened. When they told him that the prime minister of Egypt had imprisoned Simeon and demanded to see Benjamin before he would give them any more grain, Jacob was downcast. He said to them, ". . . *Me have ye bereaved of my children: Joseph is not, and Simeon is not, and ye will take Benjamin away: ALL THESE THINGS ARE AGAINST ME*" (Gen. 42:36).

Jacob thought the circumstances were against him,

but all the while God was working them out in his favor! Jacob was going to have to risk losing Benjamin in order to survive the famine, and it seemed like a terrible price to pay. But as Jacob gave in, God worked everything out to his good, and in the long run Jacob's decision to send Benjamin to Egypt paid off.

It always pays to obey God and His Word and to submit to His guidance in life. But as I said, it will cost you something to disobey.

Don't Learn Obedience the Hard Way

I know an account of a well-educated denominational preacher who enjoyed great success and fame as a traveling minister before World War I. He had published a few books and was in great demand as a speaker all over the world. He lived in a mansion in southern California and had a library worth thousands of dollars. He drove the best cars and had large savings accounts in several different banks.

This minister had gotten in on some Charismatic prayer meetings in California, where he saw the truth concerning the baptism in the Holy Ghost. He said, "I saw that God wanted me to be filled with the Holy Ghost with the evidence of speaking in other tongues.

"One night at one of these prayer meetings, as I was waiting before the Lord, the Holy Ghost came upon me, and I began to stammer and speak in other tongues.

"Then I began to think about what was happening. I thought about what my denomination believed about

Charismatics or tongue-talkers. They thought tongue-talkers were in some kind of cult.

"I thought, *What will this do to my standing in my church? What will this do to my income?* When I entertained these thoughts, the anointing left me like a bird flying away. I knew God wanted me to be filled with the Holy Ghost, but I said, 'It is too big a price to pay. I'll lose my prestige and the approval of my denomination.'

"When the anointing left me, I quietly slipped out of the meeting while no one was looking."

During his next meeting — before the month was out — this minister became very sick. And during the following two years, he spent all of his wealth on doctors and hospitals trying to get well.

The minister grew worse and worse, but doctors couldn't find out what was wrong with him. Finally, he lay dying in a charity hospital because he couldn't even pay his hospital bill. He had lost all of his great fortune and had become a charity case.

Someone asked, "Do you think God sent that sickness on him?" No! A thousand times, no! God didn't put that on him, but when you're in disobedience to God and His Word, you're on the devil's territory where he can attack you.

The minister asked his brother to put him on a train so he could go back home and spend his last days at his mother's farm in Texas. His brother had to borrow the money for a train ticket, but he sent his brother to Texas to die.

The doctors said the minister would die before he got to Texas, but he didn't. An ambulance was waiting for him at the train depot to take him to his mother's farm.

The minister rejoiced to see his mother, who was now in her eighties. Someone else farmed the land for her, and a nineteen-year-old boy lived on the farm to help her with the everyday chores. This boy became the minister's nurse because the minister had become so weak, he couldn't even turn himself over in his bed.

One day the nineteen-year-old boy said to the minister, "Reverend, why don't you let the Lord heal you?"

"What do you mean, *heal* me?" the minister asked.

"The Bible says, '*Is any sick among you? let him call for the elders of the church; and let them pray over him, anointing him with oil in the name of the Lord: And the prayer of faith shall save the sick, and the Lord shall raise him up . . .*'" (James 5:14,15).

This world-renowned minister, who had studied at a university and a seminary, asked, "Is that really in the Bible? Get me my Bible and find that scripture for me."

"I can't read," the boy replied.

"Then how come you know that's in the Bible?" the minister questioned.

"Because I heard my pastor preach on it."

"Your pastor preached from that scripture? Does he anoint people with oil and pray for them to be healed?"

"Yes."

"Then take me to him," the minister said.

Some men made a bed for that minister and put him in the back of an old Model-T Ford. They drove him out in the country to a brush-arbor meeting, where the boy's pastor was preaching. (A brush arbor is just four posts put up with a little wire over it topped with brush to keep the sun out!)

The minister related: "I could hear this pastor preaching, and afterward, he came out to the car and anointed me with oil and prayed. When he finished praying, I said, 'That's it, glory to God! I'm healed.'"

It was midnight before they got home from the meeting. They carried the minister in the house, and he said to his mother, "Momma, make me some biscuits and some of that good gravy and ham. I want something to eat."

His mother replied, "Son, you haven't had anything solid to eat in two years. You can't eat a big meal like that."

"Yes I can. God healed me."

"Well, how do you *feel?*" she asked him.

"The Bible says I'm well. According to the Word, I'm healed."

From that moment on, that minister was completely healed. He began to regain his strength and started writing articles for various magazines about his healing. Then calls began coming in for him to hold meetings.

Just before he was about to leave to speak at a city-wide meeting in a certain city, the nineteen-year-old boy who had helped him said, "Reverend, before you go, you ought to let God baptize you with the Holy Ghost."

Remembering what had happened two years before when he ran away from God and wouldn't pay the price, he said to the boy, "Yes, you're right. I'm not going anywhere to minister until God baptizes me with the Holy Ghost." And, thank God, he was baptized in the Holy Ghost and spoke with other tongues.

This minister went on to become an internationally known Full Gospel preacher. When he submitted to God and His Word, God made it up to him and restored what he'd lost. I never heard this minister preach, but I read some of his writings and they were marvelous.

Folks who knew him told me that when the time came for him to go home to be with the Lord, he just sat down and began to sing, "Swing Low, Sweet Chariot" and went on home, glory to God!

The Lord's way is always best! The Lord's way is a way of blessing, protection, and victory even in the midst of life's greatest tests and trials. It doesn't cost to obey God and His Word; it *pays*! It will pay you great dividends to obey God's Word and His plan for your life.

God's Word Is God's Will

As I said before, some Christians get so caught up trying to receive specific direction from God about what He wants them to do, they forget to be doers of the *Word*. For example, the Bible has a lot to say about forgiveness, but for some reason, many believers don't practice forgiveness the way the Bible teaches it.

The subject of forgiveness has a twofold application. In other words, you have to forgive others when they miss it, but you also have to forgive yourself when you miss it in some area of your life. If you don't learn this lesson, you'll be crippled and handicapped all the rest of your life in living for God and walking with Him.

First John 1:9 says, *"If we confess our sins, he is faithful and just to forgive us our sins, and to cleanse us from all unrighteousness."* If you've repented and confessed your sin to God, the Bible says He is faithful and just to forgive you and to cleanse you from all unrighteousness. And God will not remember that you ever did anything wrong (Isa. 43:25).

HEBREWS 8:12
12 For I will be merciful to their unrighteousness, and THEIR SINS AND THEIR INIQUITIES WILL I REMEMBER NO MORE.

Since God doesn't remember your sins, then why should you remember them? It would be in poor taste to remind God of your sins when He has forgotten them.

ISAIAH 43:25,26
25 I, even I, am he that blotteth out thy transgressions for mine own sake, and WILL NOT REMEMBER THY SINS.
26 PUT ME IN REMEMBRANCE: let us plead together: declare thou, that thou mayest be justified.

Notice verse 26: *"Put me in remembrance. . . ."* In other words, remind God of what He said in His Word.

Certainly, you need to remind God, because He commanded us to remind Him. But you need to remind *yourself* too. If you don't remind yourself of God's Word concerning the forgiveness of sin, you could fall prey to the devil's accusations that he will try to bring against you to remind you of your past and keep you in bondage to failure and defeat.

Forget the Past —
God Wants You To Succeed!

When you've confessed your sin to God and received forgiveness, the devil will invariably bring up your past as a photograph. But, after all, that's all it is — just a picture — because your sin doesn't exist anymore once you've confessed it to God. The Bible says, *"I, even I, am he that BLOTTETH OUT thy transgressions FOR MINE OWN SAKE . . ."* (Isa. 43:25).

Notice the phrase "for Mine own sake." God didn't say He would blot out your transgressions and not remember your sins for *your* sake. Don't misunderstand me, *you* would reap the benefit of God's forgiveness. But He said, "I will blot out your transgressions and not remember your sins for *My* sake." He will not remember your sins for His sake so He can bless you, help you, and demonstrate His great love and mercy on your behalf.

PHILIPPIANS 3:13,14
**13 Brethren, I count not myself to have appre-
hended: but this one thing I do, FORGETTING**

**THOSE THINGS WHICH ARE BEHIND, and reach-
ing forth unto those things which are before,
14 I press toward the mark for the prize of the
high calling of God in Christ Jesus.**

The Apostle Paul wrote this to the Philippian
Church. He was talking about himself, although these
verses apply to every believer.

Before any believer can go on with God and reach
his fullest potential in the ministry or whatever God
has called him to do, he will have to forget about the
past, especially his past mistakes.

Notice something else Paul said about himself in
writing to Timothy.

1 TIMOTHY 1:12-16
**12 And I thank Christ Jesus our Lord, who hath
enabled me, for that he counted me faithful,
putting me into the ministry;**
**13 Who was before a blasphemer, and a persecu-
tor, and injurious: but I obtained mercy, because I
did it ignorantly in unbelief.**
**14 And the grace of our Lord was exceeding abun-
dant with faith and love which is in Christ Jesus.**
**15 This is a faithful saying, and worthy of all
acceptation, that Christ Jesus came into the world
to save sinners; of whom I am chief.**
**16 Howbeit for this cause I obtained mercy, that
in me first Jesus Christ might shew forth all long-
suffering, for a pattern to them which should here-
after believe on him to life everlasting.**

Then let's read what Luke was inspired to write
about Paul, or Saul of Tarsus, in the Book of Acts.

ACTS 7:58
58 And cast him [Stephen] out of the city, and
stoned him: and the witnesses laid down their
clothes at a young man's feet, whose name was
Saul.

ACTS 8:1
1 And Saul was consenting unto his death. . . .

ACTS 9:1,2
1   And Saul, yet breathing out threatenings and
slaughter against the disciples of the Lord, went
unto the high priest,
2   And desired of him letters to Damascus to the
synagogues, that if he found any of this way,
whether they were men or women, he might bring
them bound unto Jerusalem.

Thank God, God's mercy reached Paul, and Paul got
born again and became a new creature in Christ. Second Corinthians 5:17 says, *"Therefore if any man be in
Christ, he is a new creature: OLD THINGS ARE
PASSED AWAY; behold, all things are become new."*

That's what Paul was talking about in Philippians
3:13: *". . . FORGETTING THOSE THINGS WHICH ARE
BEHIND, and reaching forth unto those things which are
before."* Through the new birth, Paul didn't have any past.
And in God's eyes, Paul stood before God completely righteous — as though sin never existed in his life.

But *Paul* had to learn to forget too. After all, it was
terrible the havoc he had wrought in the Church before
he got saved. From the Scripture we know he consented
to the death of Stephen, and he threatened other disciples of Jesus Christ.

If Paul *hadn't* learned to forget, he could have never fulfilled the call of God and stood in the office or ministry God had called him to. We, too, must learn to forget, or we won't be able to successfully follow God's plan for our own lives.

Forgive Yourself

It's just as wrong to be unwilling to forgive yourself as it is to be unwilling to forgive others. Failure to forgive others and yourself and forget the mistakes of the past will hinder you from receiving from God, from growing spiritually, and from being what God wants you to be.

Once after a meeting I held in Texas some years ago, a lady approached me as I was leaving the building, and she said, "Brother Hagin, I want you to pray for me."

"What for?" I asked her.

"Do I have to tell you?" she replied.

"Yes, I'm not going to pray for you unless you do, because I can't agree with you and have faith for something when I don't know what it is I'm believing for."

"Well, I'll tell you," she said. "But you won't laugh at me, will you?"

"No, I might laugh *with* you, but I won't laugh *at* you."

She said: "I've been born again and filled with the Holy Ghost for about eight years now. My husband is still unsaved.

"Before I got saved," she continued, "I was always hot tempered. I had a fiery temper and would have temper tantrums just at the drop of a hat.

"Awhile ago, my husband, who is a fine gentleman, came home acting like he was drunk. I got mad at him and lost my temper and began yelling at him.

"Then he hollered, 'I'm not drunk! I'm just kidding you. I thought it would be fun to come home and pretend to be drunk.'

"That made me madder than ever," this woman continued, "and then I really let him have it. I yelled and screamed at him, and then I went to our bedroom and slammed the door.

"After I cooled off a little, I was so embarrassed because of some of the things I had said. So I got down on my knees and prayed nearly all night long, 'Dear God, forgive me.'

"The next morning at the breakfast table, I said to my husband, 'Honey, I want you to forgive me. I prayed nearly all night long, and I know God says in His Word that He'll forgive me. But I want to ask you to forgive me too.'

"My husband said, 'Well, if anybody ought to ask for forgiveness, it's me. I ought to ask *you* to forgive *me*, because I started the whole thing. I'm to blame, not you.'

"We agreed to each take part of the responsibility and just forgive each other," the woman said.

I told her, "You haven't asked me anything. You just

told me something. What in the world do you need to pray about?"

"Well," she said, "I wanted you to pray that God would give me some kind of feeling so I'd know He has forgiven me."

I started laughing. I couldn't keep from it. "Why, Sister, do you know what you just got through telling me? You just told me that you've got more faith and confidence in your unsaved husband than you do in God! You asked your husband to forgive you, and he did. And that settled it for you. But you won't take God at His Word. God said, *'If we confess our sins, he is faithful and just to forgive us our sins, and to cleanse us from all unrighteousness'"* (1 John 1:9).

I continued: "When your husband said, 'I forgive you,' you didn't get on your knees and say to the Lord, 'Give me some kind of feeling so I'll know my husband has forgiven me.' No, you just accepted your husband's forgiveness. You have more confidence in your unsaved husband's word than you do in God's Word."

"I see it now," she said. "I was wrong to ask you to pray that God would give me a feeling to let me know He's forgiven me. Just forget I asked you to pray."

Just as she started to walk away, I called to her, "Come on back here. Do you know what your problem is?"

"Do you?" she asked. "I sure do."

"Tell me then."

I said to her, "You are unwilling to forgive yourself for losing your temper. God has forgiven you, your husband has forgiven you, and you have forgiven your husband. But you haven't forgiven yourself. Forgive yourself for losing your temper, and stop holding it against yourself. Pretty soon you'll feel all right. You won't have to pray that God will give you any kind of feeling."

In about two or three days, this woman came back to the meetings, and I didn't have to ask her if she had forgiven herself. Her face was radiant. It looked like a neon sign turned on in the dark! She was all smiles because she had learned to forgive *herself*.

Many Christians are unwilling to forgive themselves for mistakes of the past — for their disobedience to God and His will. Some Christians even try to punish themselves by giving up on the dream God has put in their heart to fulfill. But as I often say, it's not what mistake you've made in the past that counts; it's what you do *afterwards* that counts with God.

Remember the Apostle Paul said, *"I press toward the mark for the prize of the high calling of God in Christ Jesus"* (Phil. 3:14). But you can't press forward toward the mark until you take the first step: *". . . FORGETTING those things which are behind . . ."* (Phil. 3:13).

No matter how you may have disobeyed God in the past, God wants you to be obedient to His Word and His will for your life today. As you surrender to God's holy written Word and to His plan and purpose for your life, you will reap great dividends. In the long run, it will never cost you to obey God; it will always pay!

Chapter 7
Love's Way Is the Best Way

Love never fails. . . .

— 1 Corinthians 13:8 (*NIV*)

Do you want to successfully follow God's plan for your life and do God's will on the earth? If you want to follow a path that is guaranteed to lead you into certain victory and success in life, then follow the way of love — God's love.

The Apostle Paul said, talking about love, ". . . *yet shew I unto you a more excellent way*" (1 Cor. 12:31). Love's way is the best way — the more excellent way — because God is love, and love never fails.

Love is of the heart. It is a fruit of the recreated human spirit. Therefore, love can grow. How can a person grow and develop in God's love?

The Bible says, ". . . *the love of God is shed abroad in our hearts by the Holy Ghost which is given unto us*" (Rom. 5:5). The love of God is already in our hearts if we are born again. But we grow in love by confessing it and acting on it.

My wife and I were once holding a meeting in the western part of the nation, where we renewed acquaintances with a young couple I'd met earlier at a ministers' convention. Both the husband and wife were ordained ministers.

155

After I preached, the couple asked us to go out and have a bite to eat with them. At the restaurant, the wife of this young minister said to me, "Brother Hagin, you've got me confused."

"No," I said, "I don't have you confused. You were confused before I got here. The light of God's Word just showed it up. But what is the matter?"

She said: "In your message today, you quoted First John 3:15: *'Whosoever hateth his brother is a murderer: and ye know that no murderer hath eternal life abiding in him.'*"

"Yes, that's right," I answered. "I plead guilty. I said that."

In ministering, many times the Holy Ghost will have you say things you didn't plan on saying. Those things just come out of your spirit by the inspiration of the Holy Ghost. For instance, when I quoted First John 3:15 to the congregation, I said, "The Bible says that whoever hates his brother — that means *mothers-in-law* too — is a murderer."

"Well, I hate my mother-in-law," she continued.

I knew this woman didn't really hate her mother-in-law. Instead of letting the love of God dominate her, she was letting her human reasoning and her flesh dominate her. Walking in the flesh will get you into trouble every time.

I said to her, "Well, if you do hate your mother-in-law, you're a murderer, and you don't have eternal life abiding in you. If the life of God was in you, then the nature of God would be in you, and God's nature is love. So the love of God would be in you."

"What am I going to do?" the woman asked, desperate.

I answered: "Sister, look me in the eye and say, 'I hate my mother-in-law.' And at the same time, see what happens in your spirit — in your heart."

So she said, "I hate my mother-in-law."

"When you said that, what happened down in your spirit?"

"There's something down there 'scratching' me." she said.

"Sure it is," I told her. "It's the love of God. It's constraining you. It's trying to get your attention. But instead of yielding to that, you're just letting your mind run wild and your flesh dominate you."

"What am I going to do?" By now she was really desperate.

I said, "Act like you love your mother-in-law, because you do."

We live so much of our lives in the flesh that many times we forget that we're really spirit beings. We're not physical beings, and we're not soulish beings. We *are* a spirit; we *have* a soul; and we *live in* a body.

It would help you become more conscious of spiritual things, and the things of God would be more real to you if you'd think of yourself as a spirit being, because that's what you are (1 Thess. 5:23). In fact, it would help you to say that out loud: "I *am* a spirit; I *have* a soul; and I *live in* a body."

The Bible says, *". . . the love of God is shed abroad in our hearts by the Holy Ghost which is given unto us"* (Rom. 5:5). The love of God is shed abroad in our heart or spirit. It's not shed abroad in our soul or body.

The Love Walk in Connection With Healing

This woman invited my wife and me to their home for refreshments after the last service of the meeting I was holding. She also invited her mother-in-law.

That night at their home, the woman took us to the side and said, "You were right. I don't hate my mother-in-law. My in-laws are wonderful people. They're Christians and they love God. I realize the love of God was in me all the time. I just wasn't letting it dominate me."

This young couple had three children. The youngest child was a girl between three and four years of age.

For the first two years of her life, this little girl was in perfect physical condition. But then she began having epileptic seizures. Her parents took her to the leading medical specialists all over the world. One of the best doctors in that field ran tests on the little girl and told her parents her case was the worst he'd ever seen in thirty-eight years of medical practice.

The little girl had to take medication, but even the medication wouldn't stop the seizures; it only made them less intense. The parents were endeavoring to receive healing for their little child.

We were getting ready for church one night when this woman called and asked us to come over and pray for her little girl. The child was in the preliminary stages of another epileptic attack.

Ordinarily, we don't visit everyone who asks us, because if we did it for one, we'd have to do it for everyone, and we wouldn't have time to do anything else but pray for folks. But when God tells us to go, we obey Him and we go. That night the Lord told us to go and visit the family on our way to church.

Driving over there, the Lord spoke to me, and it was just as real to me as if someone were sitting in the back seat. It wasn't an audible voice, because my wife didn't hear it.

The Lord said, "Don't pray for the child. Don't anoint the child with oil. Don't lay hands on the child.

"When you get there, say to the mother, 'Under the Old Covenant, I said if My people walked in My statutes and kept My commandments, I would take sickness away from their midst and the number of their days I would fulfill.'"

Paraphrasing that in New Testament language, Jesus said in John 13:34, "A *new commandment I give unto you, That ye love one another; as I have loved you, that ye also love one another.*"

The Lord continued: "Then tell her that when she walks in My commandment of love, I'll take sickness away from the midst of her and the number of her days I'll fulfill. Say to her, 'You tell Satan, "Satan, I'm walking in love. Take your hands off my child!"'"

When we arrived, I did exactly as the Lord com-

manded me. I barely got the words out of my mouth
when the mother turned toward her little child and
said, "Satan, I'm walking in love. Take your hands off
my child!"

I'm a witness and my wife is a witness that as fast
as you could snap your fingers, that child's seizure
stopped right then. It stopped immediately — the very
second the child's mother said those words.

Five years later when the little girl was eight years
old, she was still healed. She was beautiful, happy, and
full of life and never did have another attack. The
mother told me that twice over the five-year period,
some minor symptoms showed up. I asked her, "What
did you do?"

"I said, 'Oh, no you don't, Satan. I'm walking in
love.'"

Somebody said, "Yes, that worked for her, but I
haven't been walking in love." She hadn't either, but
she repented and got back in walking in love.

If you get out of walking in love, get back in as fast
as you can. Every step out of love is sin. And every step
taken out of love is a step in the wrong direction. Failing to walk in love will hinder you from following God's
plan for your life.

I was healed more than fifty-five years ago in McKinney, Texas, as a Baptist boy reading Grandma's
Methodist Bible. I was raised up from a deathbed,
healed of two serious organic problems. My body was
nearly totally paralyzed because of a deformed heart,
and I had an incurable blood disease.

In fact, Dr. Robason, the fifth doctor on my case, said, "Son, I'll be honest with you. If you didn't have the deformed heart and the paralysis, this incurable blood disease alone would prove to be fatal to you."

In all these years since I received my healing, I continue to study the Word of God along the lines of faith and healing. And, of course, you can't study faith and healing without studying love, because the Bible says faith works by love. I have always made it my practice never to permit the least bit of animosity or ill-will in my heart against anyone.

I can go five to seven years at a time and, from the standpoint of experiencing any discomfort, don't even know that I have a body. The only times I've ever been attacked with sickness is when I acted foolishly and didn't take care of my body, and when I didn't walk in love.

Your body is still mortal, and you've got to take care of it. If you don't, you're giving place for sickness to attack. For example, there have been times my wife has said, "Honey, you ought to take your topcoat. You always get hot when you preach, and it's not a good idea to go out into the cold when you're hot."

Sometimes I didn't listen to her, and I did just that — I went out into the cold weather after I'd been preaching up a storm, and my throat would tighten up and begin to get sore. Then I had to repent of my stupidity first before I could get healed. But nothing has ever been seriously wrong with me in these more than fifty-five years except when I missed God and I got out of walking in love.

Walking in Love Toward God

You understand there's more than one way to get out of the love walk. Not only are we to walk in love toward one another, but we are to love God. That means we are to put Him first.

When you're in disobedience, you're not walking in love toward God. The Bible says, "*. . . Thou shalt love the Lord thy God with all thy heart, and with all thy soul, and with all thy mind*" (Matt. 22:37). At times, I've gotten out of walking in love toward God by getting into disobedience about God's plan for my life. You're not following God's plan for your life if you're not walking in love and obedience to Him.

But when I would get into disobedience, I'd run just as fast as I could to get back in love. The minute I got back in love, I was all right as quickly as you could snap your fingers.

But I had to repent just like you'll have to repent if you disobey God and His Word and walk out of love. If you're in disobedience, you know it. And if you're in disobedience, don't wait to repent. Be quick to repent and get back into love. Love's way is the best way, because love's way is God's way.

I know it's possible to walk in divine health. I've walked in divine health for more than fifty-five years. Divine health is God's will for His children.

"How do you do it?" someone asked. I walk in love. I'm not bragging on me; I'm bragging on Jesus. I'm bragging on the Word. And I want you to get to the place if you're not already there of walking in divine health. God is no respecter of persons. He doesn't favor me over you. God favors anyone who is committed to His Word.

Jesus said, *"If ye love me, keep my commandments"* (John 14:15). If you're committed to believing and doing God's Word, you'll be walking in love toward God and your fellow man. And you'll be fulfilling the Law.

ROMANS 13:8
8   Owe no man any thing, but to love one another: for he that loveth another hath fulfilled the law.

Many people take this scripture out of its setting and try to make it say we're not supposed to buy anything on credit. But that's not what this verse is saying. If you buy something on credit, you don't owe anything until the payment comes due. And if you pay it, you still don't owe anything. It's when you don't make your payments that you owe something.

If you'll study this verse carefully, you'll understand that it is really saying that you owe it others to love them, and it's a debt you'll never get paid. You've got to keep on loving others.

Love Fulfills the Law

Notice the last part of that verse. *". . . for he that loveth another hath fulfilled the law."* In other words, if you're walking in love, you're walking in God's will for your life, and it will be easy to follow His plan and purpose for you.

Think about it. Under the Old Covenant, God's people could fulfill the Law and sickness would be taken away from them and the number of their days would be fulfilled. But under the New Covenant, he who walks in love has also fulfilled the Law.

Under the New Covenant, if I could fulfill the Law, I should get the same results they did under the Old Covenant: healing and divine health. If I don't get the same results, then God would be unjust.

> **ROMANS 13:9,10**
> 9 For this, Thou shalt not commit adultery, Thou shalt not kill, Thou shalt not steal, Thou shalt not bear false witness, Thou shalt not covet; and if there be any other commandment, it is briefly comprehended in this saying, namely, Thou shalt love thy neighbour as thyself.
> 10 LOVE WORKETH NO ILL TO HIS NEIGHBOUR: THEREFORE LOVE IS THE FULFILLING OF THE LAW.

The Old Covenant had Ten Commandments. The New Covenant has one commandment. Somebody asked me, "You mean we don't have to keep the Ten Commandments?" Certainly not. If you're walking in love, you're not going to break *any* commandments. That's what Paul said in Romans 13.

If you're walking in love toward your fellow man, you're not going to kill him. If you love him, you won't tell a lie on him. In fact, the Bible says, ". . . *love covereth all sins*" (Prov. 10:12). If you see someone doing wrong, you shouldn't go tell it to others so as to expose and embarrass him. No, you should pray for him and help him, because love covers a multitude of sins.

If you walk in love, you'll never break any of the commandments that were given to curb sin. So love is the only commandment you need to concern yourself with. Love is the fulfilling of the Law.

That's the reason I said if I miss it and get out of love, I run to get back in walking in love as fast as I can, because if I walk in love, I am fulfilling the Law. And God said to those who fulfilled the Law, "I will take sickness away from your midst and the number of your days I will fulfill."

So that's one thing I've always been doubly careful about — and that is making sure that I walk in love. As I said, I never allow the least bit of animosity, ill-will, or wrong feeling in my heart toward anybody. I won't let negative feelings toward others touch me for a minute. I want to follow God's perfect plan for my life and experience His best blessings. I couldn't do that if I didn't walk in love.

An evangelist held a meeting for me one time, and there's no doubt about it — he did me wrong. I'll not tell what he did, because it wouldn't be edifying.

The devil said to my mind, "If I were you, I wouldn't take him up another offering."

When we held meetings every night, it was our custom to take offerings on Tuesday, Friday, and Sunday nights for the evangelist or guest speaker. The other nights we took up an expense offering to cover the other expenses of the meeting.

When the devil said that to my mind (I knew it was the devil, because it wasn't love, so it couldn't have been God speaking to me), I said, "Just for that, Mr. Devil, I'm going to take up an offering for him every night."

You see, the Bible says, "... *LOVE your enemies, BLESS them that curse you, DO GOOD to them that hate you, and PRAY for them which despitefully use you, and persecute you*" (Matt. 5:44). Another scripture says we are to return good for evil (1 Thess. 5:15).

So I took up an offering every night for this evangelist, even though he had done me wrong. I told the devil, "If you say anything else about him, I'll take him up *two* offerings a night." The devil never mentioned another word. He doesn't want *any* preacher to receive two offerings a night! He's mad enough about them getting *one* every night.

My church back then was smaller than some of the churches this evangelist had preached in, so I asked this evangelist how much he averaged when he preached a meeting. I gave him three times that much, and I put a third of it in myself, out of my own pocket. That's walking in love, and that's what the Bible says to do.

Do you want to stay healthy and well and be blessed and be able to successfully follow God's plan for your life? Then do what the Word says to do and walk in love.

GALATIANS 5:14
14 For ALL the law is fulfilled in one word, even in this; Thou shalt love thy neighbour as thyself.

If you're not careful on any Bible subject, you can

get into the ditch on one side of the road or the other, instead of going down the middle. For example, some folks get in the ditch over on one side, saying, "Well, we're just going to walk in love," and they never take a stand on anything.

But many times you can't help folks when you don't take a stand for something. Sometimes you need to speak the truth to them in love. Then you can teach them and help them, especially if you're a minister.

Sometimes you have to love people enough to tell them the truth — Bible truth. You see, love isn't always quiet or tolerant of sin.

Certainly, God is love. But as I said, there is a judgment side of God. Does that mean that He's not a God of love? No, God is always love, and He always does the right thing.

1 CORINTHIANS 5:1-5
1   It is reported commonly that there is fornication among you, and such fornication as is not so much as named among the Gentiles, that one should have his father's wife.
2   And ye are puffed up, and have not rather mourned, that he that hath done this deed might be taken away from among you.
3   For I verily, as absent in body, but present in spirit, have judged already, as though I were present, concerning him that hath so done this deed,
1   In the name of our Lord Jesus Christ, when ye are gathered together, and my spirit, with the power of our Lord Jesus Christ,
5   To deliver such an one unto Satan for the destruction of the flesh, that the spirit may be saved in the day of the Lord Jesus.

It wasn't God's best that this man be turned over to Satan for the destruction of his flesh. But it wasn't God's best that this fellow live in sin either. If he wouldn't judge himself and put away sin, then if Love didn't do something about it, the man would wind up in hell.

So it was really an act of God's mercy that this man be turned over to Satan for the destruction of his flesh so he would judge sin in his life and repent. Someone who has known God, but has fallen away, will usually turn back to God when his flesh starts hurting.

That's not God's best, but it sure beats going to hell. And Paul, through the love and mercy of the Holy Spirit, turned this man over to Satan to keep him from going to hell. That was love, not hate.

Obedience Is Love's Way

Suppose you had a little four-year-old boy, and you saw him playing with matches. So you reprimanded him and said, "Son, don't do that. You could burn the house down and kill yourself and others."

What if your son paid no attention to you, and two or three days later he did the same thing. This time, you'd spank him and say, "I told you not to do that. Don't do that any more."

But then a few days later, you catch him and he's already got a fire going. So you give him a good spanking this time. Only this time, he learned his lesson, and he never played with matches again.

Did you do that because you hate him? No, you did

it because you love him and you're interested in his well-being. You did it to protect him.

Sometimes a pastor has to do much the same thing with the members of his congregation. It's love for a pastor to correct his congregation if need be so people can walk in God's will for their lives.

I took the pastorate of a certain church one time. There was no order at all in that church. The young people in the church were not saved, and it was no wonder, because the parents just let their kids do whatever they wanted to do. They'd sit there and talk out loud while I was preaching. I kept talking to them gently for three or four months because I was new there, and I didn't want to cause a big disturbance.

I kept talking about how you ought to behave yourself in the house of God. Then after I was there about five months, some young people got to talking so loudly, I could hear them while I was trying to preach. Everybody was looking at them talking in the back of the auditorium.

So I stopped right in the middle of the sermon and said, "Is somebody talking?" Some folks in the congregation nodded.

"Listen!" I said, and I just shut my Bible. "Listen carefully to me." I didn't want to embarrass them, but they ought to have known better than to be talking out loud during a church service.

"Now I want to tell you something," I continued. "I've been talking to all of you about four months about talking out loud during church. Now parents, look at your watches right now, because from this very second, the next time any of your children talk out loud in church or misbehave and create a disturbance, I'm going to have them arrested for disturbing public worship, and they'll be put in jail."

You say, "Is that love?" Certainly it's love. If you let children continue to misbehave, they're liable to wind up in hell.

I continued: "I'll have them arrested, and you parents will have to pay their fine." In those days we had a county farm, and you could work off your fine if you couldn't pay it because those were Depression Days.

I said, "They'll have to work their fine off out there on the county farm unless you pay it."

In the past, the young people had been threatened for misbehaving, but nothing was ever done about it, because some of the elders had said, "Well, we've got to act in love." But the kids were still just as bad as they ever were.

I ended the service and began talking to the parents of the teenagers one by one. I walked up to one man with two deacons as my witnesses. "Brother H____, I want to speak to you personally. You heard what I said from the pulpit, but I wanted to talk to you personally. I'm going to have your daughters arrested and put in jail if they persist in disturbing worship."

This man dropped his head in shame, and then he looked up at me, tears running down his face. "Brother Hagin, you're right. This is the house of God. I've tried to talk to them and make them behave, but I can't do it."

I knew what his problem was. He would try to repri-
mand his two daughters, but the mother would let them
out the back window of the house and let them stay out
all night long. Well, when there's friction and disagree-
ment in the home, there's going to be problems.

He said, "I'm with you, Brother Hagin. Go ahead
and have them arrested. I can't pay their fine. They'll
just have to work it off on the county farm."

So then I went to another parent, a dear lady. Her
husband wasn't saved and never came to church. I said
to her, "I'm going to have M____ arrested because she's
one of the worst ones about misbehaving and talking in
church."

She said, "Brother Hagin, I try to keep an eye on my
daughter, and every time I look back there, she's behaving herself." I said, "Yes, but I'm on the platform, and
she watches you. And the minute she sees your head
turn, she straightens up and starts behaving."

"Well, every time *I* look . . ." she argued.

I said, "Do you think I'm lying to you? Just ask the
people who sit around her. You ought to have her sitting
with you on the front pew. In fact, you ought to have all
your children down there with you. The others are misbehaving, too, but she's the worst. And I'm going to
have her put in jail if she does it again. I know you can't
pay the fine. She'll have to work it off on the farm."

You say, "Is that love?" Absolutely it is, because it's
love to teach and train children. If children aren't
taught to be obedient, how are they ever going to grow
up to be obedient to God and His Word? How can they

ever successfully follow His plan for their life if they can't even obey their parents or their pastor?

This dear lady answered, "Yes, Brother Hagin, but if I have the kids sitting up front with me, I can't enjoy the service."

"Why not?" I asked.

"Well, because they're always talking and squirming around."

She had just finished telling me her children didn't talk in church!

This woman would dance in the Holy Spirit in church, and she was a blessing to the rest of the church. But I told her, "You'd be a much greater blessing to this church if you didn't dance so much and saw after your children more."

After the service was over and my wife and I had gone to bed for the night, Oretha awakened because she heard somebody crying. She got up and looked out the window and saw this dear lady sitting on the front steps of the church, crying and bawling at two o'clock in the morning.

My wife said, "I'll go out there and see about her."

I said, "No, you'll ruin everything if you do. She's trying to get our sympathy. She thinks we'll rescind what we said. She's feeling sorry for herself because I told her she'd be a greater blessing to the church if she'd have her kids sit with her and make them behave."

I also talked to another family. The husband never came into the church sanctuary. He always stayed outside. The wife was saved, filled with the Spirit, and brought her two daughters with her to church.

I went outside to talk to the husband. I took the two deacons with me, and I went up to him and said, "Mr. H____, I want to talk to you. I'm going to have your teenagers arrested for disturbing public worship if they don't straighten up and start behaving.

Mr. H____ said, "Well, there's one thing about it. You and these deacons aren't always on these church grounds." He was threatening me, so I stepped right in front of him nose to nose — all 138 pounds of me — and said, "There's one thing about it! I'm not afraid of anyone or ashamed of anything."

When I did that, he ducked his head and started talking in a different tone. He said, "You're right. You're right. But my kids aren't the only ones."

I said, "No. They're not the only ones, but they're just about the worst. Now they're all going to behave."

Did you know that in six weeks' time, we had every one of those young people saved and filled with the Holy Ghost?

What happened? Love got them. We could have let them continue to misbehave, and probably not one of them would have been saved. But we got them to the altar seeking God because they got quiet and got to listening to the Bible.

So love doesn't mean that you don't take a stand when it's necessary, because it is necessary to take a stand sometimes.

I've heard folks say about their children, "We've got to win them, so we've got to walk in love and just let them do as they please."

No sir! That's not love any more than it is to let a little child continue to play with matches! He could end up burning himself to death. Love would stop him and get him on the right road.

> **EPHESIANS 6:1-3**
> **1   Children, obey your parents in the Lord: for this is right.**
> **2   Honour thy father and mother; which is the first commandment with promise;**
> **3   That it may be well with thee, and thou mayest live long on the earth.**

I never had to spank my children a lot. But when I did, I'd read the Bible to them first, and I'd read these scriptures in Ephesians 6:1-3. I was training them to be obedient so they could successfully follow God's plans and purposes and fulfill the call of God on their lives.

I'd tell them, "Do you want it to be well with you? Those are not well days when you're sick. Don't you want to live a long time on the earth?"

"Yes," they'd say.

"Well, that's why I have to spank you. I'm not spanking you because I want to. I'm spanking you because I have your best interests at heart."

I remember when Ken was about six years old. One morning I said to him, "Son, after breakfast, I want you to empty that wastebasket."

That night after we had all prayed and read the Word together, I was studying, and Ken said to me, "Daddy, I want to talk to you." He started crying and said, "Daddy, find that scripture and read that where it talks about living a long time and not being sick and about children obeying their parents."

So I found it and read it to him. He began to cry harder and said, "I didn't empty the wastebasket this morning like you told to me to. I'm sorry."

I thought he had emptied it, but his mother had emptied it. I just saw it emptied and supposed that he did it.

But Ken said, "You told me to empty it, but I didn't. I want you to forgive me." In fact, he said, "Spank me."

I said, "No. I'm not going to spank you. I didn't tell you I was going to spank you if you didn't empty it. I just told you to empty it. No, I'm not going to spank you.

"I forgive you, son, but let's get down here on our knees and ask the Lord to forgive you." We did, and God forgave him.

God Wants You To Have His Best

You see, God has our best interests at heart too. And He'll take His stand with you sometimes if you are persisting in wrongdoing and you don't judge yourself. He knows you won't be able to follow His leading in your life if you persist in sin and wrongdoing. But the Bible says, ". . . *if we would judge ourselves, we should not be judged*" (1 Cor. 11:31).

I remember in the days of *The Voice of Healing*, there was a certain minister, about thirty-five years old, who had the biggest tent in those days and always preached to the biggest crowds. God said to me, "You go tell him that I told you to tell him that unless he judges himself, he's not going to live much longer. And the number one thing he needs to judge himself on is walking in love toward his fellow ministers."

About three years after God said that to me, he was dead because he wouldn't judge himself. Does that mean divine healing is not for us today? No, divine healing is still just as real as it ever was. I mean if an Israelite under the Old Covenant died prematurely because of sin, would that do away with the fact that God established a covenant of healing with them? No!

And under the New Covenant, just because somebody dies prematurely, that doesn't mean healing is not for us today. Healing is for everyone because love is for everyone. God wants His people healthy and to live long lives on the earth. God is love, and He is no respecter of persons. He wants us all to walk in love so we can walk in His perfect plan and live in the blessings of the New Covenant.

That young minister wouldn't judge himself, so God had to do it. God turned him over to Satan for the destruction of his flesh so that his spirit would be saved in the day of the Lord Jesus.

That wasn't God's best but it sure does beat going to hell.

People need to be taught that love's way is the best

way and that it pays to love God and obey His Word and His plan for their lives.

What does it mean to judge yourself? For example, if you miss it, say to the Lord, "I didn't walk in love in that situation. God, forgive me." And if you need to, ask the person you've sinned against to forgive you, and get back in love.

But if you're going to persist in wrongdoing and not judge yourself, sooner or later, God is going to judge you.

When you walk in love, you can walk in God's perfect plan for your life. If you haven't been walking in love, don't wait to repent and get back in the love walk. Begin walking in love and in obedience to God *today*. The rewards will be great because love's way is the best way!

It is not difficult to follow God's plan for your life. God wants you to succeed more than *you* want to. So wholeheartedly consecrate yourself to obey His Word and follow His leading in your life. If you will give God your best by walking in love and obedience to Him and His Word, you can claim God's best and live in the blessings of God in this life.

God wants every believer to run his own spiritual race and finish his course in life with joy. You *can* successfully follow and fulfill God's plan and purpose for your life.